/ 00

The Formation
of the New Testament Canon

Theological Inquiries

Studies in Contemporary
Biblical and Theological Problems

General Editor
Lawrence Boadt, C. S. P.

PAULIST PRESS
New York • Ramsey • Toronto

The Formation
of the New Testament Canon

An Ecumenical Approach

William R. Farmer
&
Denis M. Farkasfalvy, O. Cist.

Introduction by Albert C. Outler
Essays edited by Harold W. Attridge

PAULIST PRESS
New York • Ramsey • Toronto

Library of Congress
Catalog Card Number: 82-62417

ISBN: 0-8091-2495-5

Published by Paulist Press
545 Island Road, Ramsey, N.J. 07446

Printed and bound in the
United States of America

CONTENTS

THE EARLY DEVELOPMENT
OF THE NEW TESTAMENT CANON
by Denis Farkasfalvy, O. Cist.

CONTRIBUTORS TO THIS VOLUME

FR. DENIS FARKASFALVY was born in Hungary in 1936 and earned his S.T.D. from the University of St. Anselm in Rome. In 1962 he joined the Cistercian monastery "Our Lady of Dallas." He received an M.S. degree in mathematics in 1965 and began to teach religion and mathematics at the Cistercian Preparatory School in Irving, Texas, where he also served as headmaster from 1969 to 1981. Since 1965 he has taught theology at the University of Dallas. His publications include his dissertation on the concept of inspiration in St. Bernard, various articles on the biblical theology of St. Bernard, Irenaeus and the early history of the New Testament Canon. He has published in Hungarian a new translation of the Psalms, a theological introduction to biblical study and an exploration of the theology of spirituality.

PROF. WILLIAM R. FARMER was born in 1921 and was educated at Occidental College, Cambridge University and Union Theological Seminary. Since 1959 he has been on the faculty of Perkins School of Theology, Southern Methodist University, teaching courses in New Testament. He has long been active in the Society of Biblical Literature and the Society for New Testament Studies. Well known for his studies of the Jewish historical background to the New Testament and the Synoptic Problem, Dr. Farmer has also contributed numerous articles to journals and reference works dealing with questions of New Testament interpretation and early Christian history. His most recent publication is *Jesus and the Gospel* (Fortress Press, 1982). At present he is engaged in research on the rules of faith in Irenaeus and Tertullian and their relationship to scripture and the early creeds.

PROF. HAROLD W. ATTRIDGE, editor of the essays in this volume, is Associate Professor of New Testament at Perkins School of Theology, with special interests in the relationship between Judaism and early Christianity and in the history of Gnosticism.

PROF. ALBERT OUTLER is Professor of Theology emeritus at Perkins School of Theology. He has published extensively on the history of Christian doctrine and has long been active in ecumenical endeavors.

PREFACE

The two essays included in this volume represent the results of discussions held in the Seminar on the Development of Catholic Christianity, an interdisciplinary, interdenominational seminar composed of faculty members from seminaries and universities in North Texas. Since its inception some sixteen years ago, this seminar has served as a forum for wide-ranging consideration of issues relating to the development of Christianity in its classical forms. Because the topic of "canon criticism" is of such current interest in various circles, the authors of these two essays felt it appropriate to lay before a wider audience the results of their research and reflection. As chairman of the seminar during part of the period when these discussions developed, I was happy to serve in an editorial capacity for this volume, which, it is hoped, will stimulate further discussion of the sort that these essays have already generated among the immediate colleagues of Professor Farmer and Fr. Farkasfalvy.

Harold W. Attridge

INTRODUCTION

Church life in Texas has, from its beginnings, had a strong denominational bent, and this has been reflected in the patterns of theological education in the region. My first impression of Texas seminaries, in 1951, was that of separated monads, some with fewer windows than others. There were, of course, friendships and collaborations across denominational lines, but these occurred more by happenstance than by design. The situation began to change in the 1950's with the establishment of a small but short-lived joint-faculty seminar. In 1958, the Council of Southwest Theological Schools was chartered and still continues its support and sponsorship of a variety of cooperative projects. In 1975 the Southwest Commission on Religious Studies was formed to serve as coordinating agent for various interdisciplinary study projects. All of these were positive developments, but the most active and fruitful experiment of this kind has been a self-initiated, self-sustaining "Seminar in the Development of Catholic Christianity," comprised of members from seven faculties, ranging from Roman Catholic to Southern Baptist to Church of Christ.

The purpose of this seminar, begun in 1966, was to bring together scholars from the traditionally separated fields of "New Testament," "patristics," and "Church history" and to engage them in cross-disciplinary studies and discussions that would overreach traditional demarcations. We chose the "second century" as our focus, since it was an obvious "test-case" for such an experiment in boundary crossings. The dividends from this point over the past fifteen years have been more than anyone expected. There has been a notable enlargement of comradeship in inquiry and in "continuing" education—for faculty! More visible results may be seen in our harvest of published articles, chapters and books. Even a new and exciting journal, *The Second Century,* has now been launched. Thus, it is as another of the Seminar's bonuses that this volume, written by two charter members, is presented.

As different as they are, these two studies are good examples of the Seminar's spirit and quality. Here is a balanced emphasis upon research and critical analysis, together with a special concern for the questions that lie *between* "New Testament" *and* "Church history." They are addressed to a general thoughtful audience; they are instructive in focusing on an old topic (the New Testament canon), although they view it in a new perspective. Methodologically, "canon-criticism" is an extrapolation in the extended series of critical approaches to the New Testament (e.g., form-, redaction-, genre-criticism and the like). In "canon-criticism," however, the angle of vision is retrospective; the subject matter is the canonical New Testament *as a whole*. Its concern is more with the emergence of a "canon" than with its *closure*. It is more interested in the "logic" and motivations of canon-making than with its final outcome. In place of a conventional preoccupation with *disjecta membra* of New Testament texts, on the one hand, or with the elusive goal of a definitive *systematic* "theology of the New Testament," on the other, canon criticism focuses upon the *idea* of a canon and on the processes of its formation. Most of all, it is concerned with the canon's normative functions—the circumstances and issues in the second century that called it forth, and its role in the resolutions of those issues. On its historical side, it sees the emergent canon as an ecclesial antidote to various aberrant interpretations of the "apostolic message." On the sociological side, the canon is seen to have served Christianity as a safeguard against the pressures toward assimilation into the inviting religious syncretisms of the Hellenistic world.

Our first essay is by a New Testament scholar best known thus far for his studies in "The Synoptic Problem." Here, however, he ventures far beyond his field as conventionally defined and turns Church historian to good effect. In so doing, he is exemplifying one of the Seminar's special emphases. Reading backward from Eusebius, Professor Farmer has produced a dramatic reconstruction of the crisis-points in the canon-making process with flashbacks to illuminate the process as such. He seeks to redefine the roles of Marcion and of the Gnostics—and so also the tasks of the "orthodox" defenders of "Catholic faith." His most striking "discovery" concerns the

New Testament's special emphasis on "martyrdom" and its reflections in the resultant "logic" of canon-making. He is interested in the ways in which the New Testament, in its canonical form, met the needs of a *religio illicita* for the fortification of the faith of its believers in a hostile world. It is in this light that the centrality, in each of the Gospel accounts, of the *martyrdom* of Jesus is seen to make more sense than otherwise. Thus, Farmer sees the New Testament entire as "a canon for *martyrs*" (in both senses of that term).

The second essay here is by a Hungarian-born Cistercian monk, whose doctoral dissertation was on St. Bernard's use of Scripture and whose academic avocation is the teaching of mathematics! Here he turns patrologist and philologian to ponder the *idea* of a canon and its "logic." In his ponderings, he focuses on the key concept of "apostolicity," especially as this was understood by St. Irenaeus. Fr. Farkasfalvy finds an *idea* of "canon" as part of the latent canon of the Church's unfolding development. In essence, "apostolicity" is the appeal to the apostles as a group (including St. Paul of course) as the original company of authoritative witnesses (martyrs!) to the Gospel. The canon, then, is a definitive communication of Christianity's originative message in a mode designed to insure its permanent lodgment in the Christian community as its primordial authority. "Apostolicity" does not, therefore, imply some simplistic claim as to "apostolic authorship" of this New Testament book or that; it is, instead, a quite self-conscious signification of apostolic authority. Fr. Farkasfalvy shows in detail how, in the Christian lexicon, the phrase "prophets and apostles" served as a bridge-concept for the all-important continuity between, and an integration of, the Old and New Testaments. This sense of continuity helped shape the logic of canon-making "from the first Christian generation on down to the time of Irenaeus and Tertullian." Thus, the canonical New Testament provides an open access to the apostolic message in its original and true essence. This understanding of "apostolicity" was to be efficacious for the Church in any ensuing crisis of identity—and thus a perennial norm for its self-authentication. A crucial corollary derives from the fact of the New Testament's unity-in-diversity: this, too, may be seen as of the essence of true catholicity.

Farmer's essay is, by design, more "historical" than "systematic" (though not exclusively so). His narrative account of the canonical process is at least credible and provocative. Farkasfalvy's essay is more "systematic" than "historical" (though, again, not exclusively so). He shows us how the *idea* of canon, guided by the principle of apostolicity, functioned "in the movement from oral tradition to written documents" that were then established as "a perennial authority for the settling of doctrinal questions." His demonstration of this "function" in St. Irenaeus is especially thorough and convincing.

Despite their different emphases, both authors agree on the crucial role of Marcion in the canon-making process. Farmer endeavors to fathom Marcion's motives—"his all-out effort to persuade the Church to disown its Jewish heritage." Farkasfalvy is more impressed by Marcion as "the first Christian writer to present a *closed* canon . . ." (and so to raise the thorny question as to what would be *excluded* and why). Both authors thus manage to remind us of how badly we need a really adequate study of Marcion, in redress of the imbalances in both our conventional thumbnail sketches and in Harnack's famous monograph.

Both authors agree that "a canon in principle was operative in the Catholic community shortly after the middle of the second century." They join in rejecting the Enlightenment ideal of "a canon within the canon," based as it was on the hope of a discovery of a single historically demonstrable stratum of the "most primitive apostolic witness" (a project oft attempted but never yet concluded). There is, however, no mistaking Farmer's Protestant provenance (including his heritage of Enlightenment historiography) or Fr. Farkasfalvy's manifest Roman Catholic background. This, however, goes with the genius of ecumenical collaboration, since neither essay is what it would have been apart from such colleagueship.

Some of us might have wished for a more explicit analysis of *the initial crisis* that drove the tragic wedge between synagogue and Church and led to the ensuing schism that never yet has been healed. We need to know more about this than we do and what it had to do with the production of the documents that were thereafter shaped into the canon—and what it had to do with the shaping process. This, as I know, is a huge problem and sadly underdeveloped. But it is crucial for a clearer understanding of the vicissitudes of canon-making and also as a basis for the Christian-Jewish dialogue in our own time.

Even so, these two essays have afforded me much personal satisfaction on several counts, both for what they have taught me and what they exemplify of a process that I believe is of the essence of ecumenism. This they do with their demonstrations of the presence within the New Testament canon of unity-in-diversity as "normal" and normative. Farmer's notion of "the canon of martyrs" has a new relevance for Christianity in a difficult future. Farkasfalvy's ideas of "apostolicity" opens a way beyond the older quarrels about the normative status of Scripture. Closer to home, they are heartwarming signs of progress achieved in a half-generation by such experiments in ecumenical scholarship and their contribution to new levels of *koinonia* in Christ that none of us had dared foretell.

Albert C. Outler

ABBREVIATIONS

Adv. Haer.	*Adversus Haereses*
Adv. Marc.	*Adversus Marcionem*
Adv. Val.	*Adversus Valentinianos*
BJRL	*Bulletin of the John Rylands Library*
CBQ	*Catholic Biblical Quarterly*
CCL	Corpus Christianorum Latinorum
E.H.	*Ecclesiastical History*
GCS	Griechische Christliche Schriftsteller
HTR	*Harvard Theological Review*
NTS	*New Testament Studies*
PG	Patrologia Graeca
SC	Sources chrétiennes
TU	Texte und Untersuchungen
USQR	*Union Seminary Quarterly Review*

A STUDY OF THE DEVELOPMENT
OF THE NEW TESTAMENT CANON

by
William R. Farmer

INTRODUCTION

The task of discussing the topic "The Development of the New Testament Canon" must be distinguished from the task of discussing the topic "The Composition of the New Testament Books." The New Testament books belong generically to the field of early Christian literature. The task of explaining the development of the New Testament canon is the task of offering a credible account of how certain books emerged from a much larger field of early Christian literature into an ecclesiastical canon.

One could begin discussing the development of the New Testament canon by treating the composition of some particular New Testament book which in itself represents an important stage in the development of the New Testament canon. I am convinced that one could do this with Galatians, Matthew, Luke-Acts, Mark, or 2 Peter with distinctive advantage in each particular case. But that is not the method that has been followed in this study.

The point of departure for this study has been the *Vita Constantini* and *Ecclesiastical History* of Eusebius, bishop of Caesarea. The methodology has been to work backward from the closing of the canon in the fourth century to its formation in the second and its beginnings in the first. This method has the advantage of moving from the known to the unknown.

We know that the New Testament canon was defined officially for the Roman Catholic Church at the Council of Trent. We know

7

that this same New Testament canon is accepted by all the Churches which accept the Council of Chalcedon. And we know that even those Christian Churches which do not accept Chalcedon have a New Testament canon that includes all but a few of the twenty-seven books canonized at Trent. What we do not know is why the non-Chalcedonian Churches have a somewhat different New Testament canon from that of the Chalcedonian Churches, and, more important, why all Christian Churches agree at the very least on the same four Gospels, the same Acts of the Apostles, the same fourteen-letter Pauline corpus (including Hebrews), 1 Peter, and 1 John.

By what historical process did these particular books emerge from the much larger field of Christian literature as the Churches' New Testament canon? The answer that has been suggested by working backward from the fourth century to the first is this: The New Testament canon is a martyr's canon which can be traced through Origen, Hippolytus, and Irenaeus to a particular traditional idealization of Christian martyrdom exemplified by Polycarp and Ignatius and reflecting the influence of the martyrdoms of Peter and Paul in Rome. In this tradition the letters of Paul have always been united with books which witness to and emphasize the reality of the death as well as the resurrection of Jesus Christ.

On the basis of my reading of the evidence there were three major factors that contributed to the shaping of the New Testament canon. First, there was persecution of Christians. This not only evoked martyrdom, but also stimulated a whole set of responses by the Church to strengthen the faith and discipline of its members. Second, there were diverse systems of Christian theology. This doctrinal diversity, especially where it affected the question of martyrdom, tended to weaken the collective witness of Christians in the face of state persecution by denying them the added support that comes from ecclesiastical and doctrinal unity. The only state that could sustain a prolonged and widespread persecution of the Church was the Roman empire, and the only authority that could assure the Church widespread protection from such persecution was the emperor. Thus, the third major factor that contributed to the shaping of the New Testament, and especially to its acquiring its official function as a set body of documents (a closed canon), was the establishment of the

Christian religion in the Roman empire under Constantine (306–337).

A. *The Final Phase: The Closing of the Canon*

When we speak about the closing of the canon we should make a distinction between the Chalcedonian and the non-Chalcedonian Churches. The topic, "the closing of the canon," has primary reference to the final phase in the development of the New Testament as it is accepted in those branches of the Christian Church which acknowledge the validity of the Council of Chalcedon (451 A.D.). This distinction does not rest on any known decision or finding of that Council, but rather on the fact that the earlier (pre-Constantinian) diversity in the number and names of the New Testament books continues among the non-Chalcedonian Churches until the present. For example, the official New Testament canon of the Syrian Christian Churches, specifically the so-called "Jacobite" Churches, is that of the Peshitta, a Syriac version of the New Testament dating from about the fifth century. This is a twenty-two book canon and does not include the Book of Revelation, nor 2 Peter, nor 2 or 3 John, nor Jude.[1]

It is of the greatest importance to recognize that the New Testament as it is generally accepted in all branches of the Christian Church which accept the Council of Chalcedon was not finally agreed upon until the time of Constantine or shortly thereafter. De facto, of course, all the books finally included in this New Testament were recognized as Scripture in many, if not most, parts of the Church long before. But the status of Hebrews, Revelation, 2 Peter, James, Jude, 2 and 3 John was still being disputed in some important Churches right up until the time of Constantine.

1. THE NEW TESTAMENT LISTS OF
ATHANASIUS AND AMPHILOCHUS

The New Testament canon that prevailed within the Chalcedonian Churches can be traced back as far as Athanasius (296–373). His list reads as follows: Four Gospels: According to Matthew, According to Mark, According to Luke, According to John; The Acts of the Apostles; Seven Catholic Letters of the Apostles: James, Peter (1, 2), John (1, 2, 3), Jude; Fourteen Letters of Paul the Apostle: Romans, Corinthians (1, 2), Galatians, Ephesians, Philippians, Colossians, Thessalonians (1, 2), Hebrews, Timothy (1, 2), Titus, Philemon; the Revelation of John.[2]

These are precisely the books that have been universally accepted in the Chalcedonian Churches, and, except for the place of Hebrews which eventually was put after Philemon, and except for the reversed order of the Catholic letters and the letters of Paul, this is the exact arrangement of these books that eventually prevailed.[3]

The list of Amphilochus, bishop of Iconium, who died in 394, includes the same books listed by Athanasius. But Amphilochus arranged these books in the order that eventually prevailed, Hebrews after Philemon and the Catholic epistles after Paul.[4]

Amphilochus recognized that there was some question about Hebrews and listed it at the end of the Pauline corpus. But he rejected the view of those who regarded it as uncanonical. Of the Catholic letters, Amphilochus recognized that not all Church Fathers agreed on the number, some saying seven, others accepting only three, i.e., one of James, one of Peter and one of John. Amphilochus knew that some accepted the Revelation of John, but that the majority called it unacceptable. Amphilochus was obviously working with a list identical with the one that eventually achieved unquestioned acceptance in the vast majority of Chalcedonian Churches.

2. EUSEBIUS' WITNESS ON THE CANON

In his *Ecclesiastical History,* Eusebius (who died in 340) documented the state of the New Testament canon that prevailed in his own day.

> ... We must set in the first place, the holy quaternion of the Gospels, after which comes the writing of the Acts of the Apostles. After this should be reckoned the Epistles of Paul. Following them should be recognized the Epistle of John, called the first, and, likewise, the Epistle of Peter. In addition to these we should list, if it seem appropriate, the Revelation of John, the arguments concerning which

we will set forth at a proper time. These writings belong to the Recognized Books.

Of the Disputed Books, which are, nevertheless, known to the majority (and therefore can hardly be said to be "inauthentic"), there is extant the Epistle of James, as it is called; and that of Jude, and the Second Epistle of Peter; and the so-called Second and Third Epistles of John which may be the work of the evangelist or some other of the same name.

Among the books which are (not only "disputed" but should be counted as clearly) "inauthentic" are the Acts of Paul; the work entitled the Shepherd; the Apocalypse of Peter; and, in addition to them, the Epistle of Barnabas; and the so-called Teachings of the Apostles. And, in addition, as I said, the Revelation of John, if this view prevails. For, as I said, some reject it, but others give it a place among the Recognized Books.

Eusebius notes that among the "inauthentic" books some Christians reckoned also the Gospel of the Hebrews, and then continues:

Now, all these would be included among the Disputed Books; but nevertheless, we have been constrained to list them also, distinguishing between those writings, which, according to the tradition of the Church, are true, genuine and recognized (i.e., the Recognized Books), and those which differ from them in that though they are not canonical—but, rather, are disputed—are yet, nevertheless, recognized by most writers in the Church. (And this we have done) in order that we might be able to know these "disputed" writings as well as the writings which the heretics put forward in the name of the apostles, namely Gospels like those attributed to Peter, and Thomas, and Matthias, and others as well; or Acts such as those of Andrew and John and the other apostles. None of these latter books has been deemed worthy of any kind of mention in a writing by a single member of successive generations of churchmen. Moreover, the type of phraseology differs from apostolic style, and the opinion and tendency of their contents is widely dissonant from the true orthodoxy and clearly shows that they are the forgeries of heretics. For this reason, this latter group of writings ought not even to be reckoned among the books that (as designated above) are categorized as (merely) "inauthentic," but rather, should be shunned as altogether wicked and impious.[5]

Later in the same book, Eusebius, in a summary statement, writes as follows:

We have now described the facts which have come to our knowledge concerning the apostles and their times: (1) the sacred writings which they left us; (2) those books which are disputed yet, nevertheless, are publicly read by many in most churches; (3) and those which are altogether "inauthentic" and foreign to apostolic orthodoxy.[6]

This summary statement clarifies the somewhat ambiguous grouping of books that Eusebius has made. He is clearly thinking in terms of three categories. The first includes books that are accepted in all, or most, of the churches which Eusebius regards as holding the apostolic and orthodox faith. The third clearly is made up of books that are *not* cited in the writings of churchmen who stand in the succession of apostolic orthodoxy. The second category of books is less homogeneous. The books it includes are publicly read in apostolic and orthodox Churches, yet, for some reason, are disputed. Among these books are some that are sometimes grouped with the books in the first category. Eusebius will not say that they are altogether "inauthentic." Yet, they are unquestionably "disputed," a less pejorative designation. These books include James, Jude, 2 Peter, and 2 and 3 John. As for the Revelation of John, Eusebius is willing to grant that it is not only "disputed" but may be, as some claim, "inauthentic." Other "inauthentic" books that are being publicly read in apostolic and orthodox churches include the *Acts of Paul,* the *Shepherd of Hermas,* the *Apocalypse of Peter,* the *Epistle of Barnabas,* and the *Teachings of the Apostles.*

Hebrews, interestingly enough, is not specifically mentioned here by Eusebius. We know for a fact, however, that Hebrews was definitely a "disputed" book, widely rejected in the West, both before and after Eusebius. Just how settled some of these questions were may be gauged from another citation from Goodspeed's discussion:

In the West, on the other hand, the uncertainty attached not to the Revelation, but to Hebrews. We have seen that in the middle of the third century, when Roman Christianity began to use Latin, it still omitted Hebrews from the Letters of Paul, and accepted only three Catholic letters—1 Peter and 1 and 2 John. . . . Jerome, the great reviser of the Latin Bible, included it (Hebrews) in his famous Vulgate version undertaken in 382, but repeatedly mentions the Latin suspicion of it: "The custom of the Latins does not accept it." "Among the Romans, to this day, it is not considered Paul's." Augustine at first considers it Paul's, but later calls it anonymous. Yet, he does not question its place in the canon, and acknowledges that the example of the Eastern Churches has influenced him to accept it. He, in turn, influenced the North African Councils of Hippo (393) and Carthage (397, 419) to include it in their New Testament lists. . . .

The Eastern list of seven Catholic letters came even more slowly into general acceptance in the West. . . . Jerome is careful to observe that 2 and 3 John are ascribed not to John the Apostle, but to John the presbyter of Ephesus. But, as with Hebrews, his inclusion of them in his Vulgate version outweighed these halting reservations. . . . His revised New Testament of twenty-seven books undertaken at the instance of Pope Damasus, and thus having behind it the prestige of the Roman Church, completed the victory of Hebrews and the longer list of Catholic letters in the West.[7]

The order and content of Eusebius' New Testament, including its uncertainties, can be represented as follows: Four Gospels: According to Matthew, According to Mark, According to Luke, According to John; The Acts of the Apostles; (Fourteen?) Letters of Paul: Romans, Corinthians (1, 2), Galatians, Ephesians, Philippians, Colossians, Thessalonians (1, 2), Hebrews (?), Timothy (1, 2), Titus; (Two or Seven) Catholic Letters of the Apostles: Epistle of Peter (1, 2?), Epistle of John (1, 2, and 3?), (James?), (Jude?); (Revelation of John?). There is no reason to doubt that Eusebius included Philemon as an undisputed letter of Paul. But, since he does not actually list Paul's letters, we cannot be sure whether Philemon would be listed with the letters addressed to Churches, possibly immediately following Colossians, with which it is closely connected, or grouped with Timothy (1, 2) and Titus as a letter addressed to an individual. Both Athanasius and Amphilochus list Philemon just after Titus.

The overall order of these books is important. Paul's letters follow Acts and come before the Catholic letters, as in the arrangement of the New Testament canon that finally prevailed. Since Athanasius places the Catholic letters before the letters of Paul, and since there is strong manuscript support for this arrangement going back to fourth-century Egypt,[8] the reverse arrangement, where the letters of Paul are given pride of place among the letters of the apostles, seems significant.[9]

B. *The Alexandrian School*

Origen's New Testament canon is very close to that which was later adopted by Eusebius and Athanasius. But, if we go behind Origen in the Alexandrian School, back to his predecessor Clement, we find a somewhat different situation. What were the sources of this difference? One source was the diverging perception of martyrdom held by Clement and Origen. For Clement, martyrdom was not as important as it was for Origen.

In his introduction to Origen's *Exhortation to Martyrdom*, Henry Chadwick has written:

> Only the martyr, felt Origen, truly followed Christ and was in union with him. The disciple who takes up his cross and follows Jesus attains, he says, to an immediate knowledge of God whom he sees face to face.[10]

Chadwick goes on to say:

> This is a belief fundamental to Origen's ideas about the nature of the Church and of the spiritual life. It is for this reason that Origen's *Exhortation to Martyrdom* is so moving a document, and tells us so much of the spirit of the early Church.[11]

Robert Grant, in his chapter on "Alexandria and the New Testament," after crediting Origen with a decisive role in creating the final form of the New Testament canon, notes:

> Of course he did not do so in isolation from the Churches in which he taught. But his achievement means that in the shaping of the canon the theological and the literary historical factors were inseparable.[12]

As we assess the contribution of the Alexandrian school to the development of the New Testament, it will be important to focus on martyrdom as a central theological problem for the early Church.[13]

In opening his discussion of "The Age of Origen," Edgar Goodspeed writes: "He lived in an age of persecution."[14] Goodspeed notes that Origen's public career began during the persecution of Septimius Severus in A.D. 202, and that Origen died in A.D. 254 in the aftermath of the Decian persecution.

The year A.D. 202 marks a watershed in the history of the Church in Alexandria. Clement, who, before the persecution which broke out in that year, had expounded a "soft" view of Christian martyrdom,[15] left Alexandria during the persecution, and the bishop of Alexandria, after Clement's departure, put in his place, as head of the catechetical school, an eighteen-year-old student of Clement, who, by contrast, through word and deed, set forth a "very firm," if not a "hard" view of Christian martyrdom.[16] This was a very dramatic and far-reaching move on the part of the bishop of the Church in Alexandria, and it signaled a not unimportant change in the religious climate of the Christian community in Egypt. Origen's father was arrested during the early stages of the persecution. The son, unable to reach his father in prison, sent him a letter encouraging him not to deny his faith out of concern for his family. Origen almost certainly carried with him throughout his life the firm conviction that his father had made a faithful confession, and that his father's martyrdom, and that of his friends, and subsequently that of some of his students deserved a more effective and a theologically sounder scriptural defense than the views of his teacher Clement made possible.

An opportunity to address himself to this task came after Origen had left Alexandria and had settled in Caesarea in Palestine. In A.D. 235, another persecution against the Church broke out. This persecution was aimed at the leadership of the Church. Only the clergy were attacked. Origen addressed his *Exhortation to Martyrdom* to his wealthy patron, Ambrose, who was in deacons' orders, and to Protoctetus, a presbyter of the Church at Caesarea.

It was Ambrose who had financed most of Origen's literary and historical research and urged Origen to write commentaries on the Scriptures. The very task of deciding which books to write commentaries on would have entailed for both Origen and Ambrose the question of which books were regarded as canonical. So, here in his *Exhortation to Martyrdom,* addressed to his publisher and friend, we have an illustration of just how "inseparable" were "the theological and literary historical factors" which served to shape the New Testament canon.

Before examining Origen's *Exhortation to Martyrdom* to see what it can tell us about the development of the New Testament canon, we must first survey the New Testament canons of Clement and Origen, noting where they agree and where they diverge from one another. Then we will consider these agreements and differences in relation to the New Testament canon of a contemporary of Clement and Origen who was teaching and writing in another part of the Roman empire. Finally, in the light of all this evidence, we will evaluate the effect of the significant shift that took place in the Alexandrine school during the persecution of Severus when Origen was appointed to replace Clement as head of the single most influential catechetical school in Christendom.

The "five-decade career" of Origen spans the half-century during which the earlier scriptural pluralism of some Churches was weighed in the balance and found wanting. Earlier Catholic achievements were consolidated and further refined in the continuing fires of heresy and persecution. The earlier achievements had been made in other parts of the Church: in Asia Minor, Rome and Gaul. But Alexandria in Egypt and Caesarea in Palestine, under Origen's influence, will be seen to have helped in shaping the final form of the New Testament, both by critical reflection and by passion.

1. THE NEW TESTAMENT CANON OF CLEMENT (150– c. 215)

Clement had traveled widely before settling down in Egypt. He had been in Palestine, Greece and Italy. Thus, he certainly knew what Scriptures were being used in the Christian Churches in all those places. It should come as no surprise then to learn that Clement's New Testament included most, if not all, the books that eventually were included in the canon of the Chalcedonian Churches.[17] The three possible or probable exceptions are James, 3 John and 2 Peter. Clement's New Testament included: Matthew, Mark, Luke, and John, which he recognized as having been the Gospels handed down in the Church, and which he cited far more often than he did three other Gospels, the *Gospel of the Hebrews,* the *Gospel of the Egyptians* and the *Gospel of Mattathias;* Acts of the Apostles; Fourteen Letters of Paul, including Hebrews; 1 Peter; 1 and 2 John; Jude; *1 Clement,* which he cites as from an apostle; *Barnabas,* which he cites as from an apostle; the *Preaching of Peter;* the *Revelation of Peter;* the *Didache;* the *Shepherd of Hermas;* the Revelation of John. This is a conservative list of Clement's New Testament. He certainly knew and used other Christian writings. But that he regarded these as Scripture is not clear. Other books in this category listed by Stählin include the *Protoevangelium of James,* the *Acts of John* and the *Acts of Paul.*[18] Goodspeed notes, "On the whole, Clement's canon of Christian Scripture was not well-defined."[19] But if we pay attention to the frequency with which Clement refers to the thirty-six books listed above, it is clear that he is using basically the same New Testament that was being used elsewhere in the Church. The major exception is his frequent use of Hebrews, not included in the New Testaments of his contemporaries in other parts of the Church, and his relatively frequent use of the epistles of *Barnabas* and *1 Clement,* both of which he cited as from apostles, as well as his high regard for the *Shepherd of Hermas,* which he clearly accepted as inspired. Matthew, Mark, Luke, and John are very important to Clement as are Paul's letters, including the Pastorals and Hebrews. Jude is important to Clement, as is 1 John and 1 Peter. The Revelation of John and the Acts of the Apostles seem relatively less important to him.

2. THE NEW TESTAMENT CANON OF ORIGEN (185–254)

Like Clement, Origen also traveled widely. His travels carried him to Arabia, and to Greece, and as far north and east as Cappadocia, and as far west as Rome. The effect of Origen's contacts with Churches outside Egypt upon his reflection about the New Testament canon was to make him aware that some of the books his teacher Clement had used as Scripture were not used or accepted as Scripture in certain other Churches. There was, to be sure, a major corpus of Christian Scriptures accepted in most, if not all, Churches. This included: Matthew, Mark, Luke, John, Acts of the Apostles, thirteen letters of Paul, 1 Peter, 1 John, and the Revelation of John. It appears that while Origen was still in Alexandria, he accepted as canonical the *Didache,* the *Shepherd of Hermas,* and the *Epistle of Barnabas,* but after settling in Caesarea, he became aware that these books were not accepted there. He also developed doubts concerning the *Preaching of Peter,* which Clement had liked. Origen continued to accept *Barnabas* and the *Shepherd of Hermas,* as well as Jude, 2 and 3 John, James, and 2 Peter, even though he realized that they were disputed in some Churches. Origen went out of his way to defend the apostolic character of Hebrews and used it as one of Paul's letters, even though he realized that it probably was not actually written by Paul. Origen clearly rejected some books, like the *Gospel of Thomas,* the *Gospel of Mattathias,* the *Gospel of the Twelve,* the *Gospel of the Egyptians,* and the *Acts of Paul.*[20]

Origen and Clement agree on the undisputed canonical status of twenty-two books. These are: Matthew, Mark, Luke, John, Acts of the Apostles, fourteen letters of Paul, including Hebrews, 1 Peter, 1 John, and the Revelation of John. There are five books which Clement treats as canonical and which Origen accepts, but with the proviso that they are "disputed." These are: Jude, Clement, *Barnabas, Shepherd of Hermas,* and 2 John. There are three books which Origen accepts with the proviso that they are "disputed" and which seem not to have been used or known to Clement: 3 John, James, 2 Peter. There are some books which Clement accepted but which Origen did not accept. These include *The Preaching of Peter, The Revelation of Peter, The Gospel of the Egyptians, The Gospel of Mattathias,* and possibly *The Gospel of the Hebrews.* The *Didache,* which Origen originally accepted at Alexandria should also be included in this list.

3. THE NEW TESTAMENT CANON OF HIPPOLYTUS (d. 235)

Edgar Goodspeed, at the close of his discussion of Origen's contribution to the formation of the New Testament, makes the following observation:

> When Origen, as a young man still in his twenties visited Rome [c. 210–215], he listened to the preaching of Hippolytus. Precocious as Origen was, he was still a youth beside the great Hippolytus, then at the height of his powers, and the picture of the great genius of Eastern Christianity, sitting under the preaching of his greatest Western contemporary, is one to stir the imagination. They must have met and had some conversation, and certainly this Roman visit cannot have been without influence upon the active mind of Origen.[21]

The evidence [not cited by Goodspeed] that Origen heard the great Roman theologian Hippolytus preach in Rome comes from Jerome.[22] But Jerome tells us more than that. Jerome informs us that among the works of Hippolytus was an exhortation, "On the Praise of Our Lord and Savior." It would appear that Jerome had read this sermon carefully for he writes that in this sermon Hippolytus "indicates that he is speaking in the Church in the presence of Origen." Thus, Hippolytus was not only aware of the presence of Origen in the congregation, but he took the opportunity to recognize this publicly. Something else that Jerome tells us in the same place suggests that this was no chance meeting. We are informed that the wealthy and influential deacon of Alexandria, Ambrose, had urged Origen to emulate Hippolytus in writing commentaries on the Scriptures, and in this connection had offered him "seven and even more secretaries, and their expenses, and an equal number of copyists." This certainly would have provided a motive for Origen to make contact with the learned Roman theologian while he was in Rome, and it could possibly have been one of his main reasons for making the trip to Rome.

In any case, Hippolytus was an important witness to the New Testament as understood in Rome in a formative period of Origen's career, and Origen did make contact with him.

Goodspeed numbers the books of Hippolytus' New Testament canon as twenty-two. These are: Matthew, Mark, Luke, John, Acts of the Apostles, thirteen letters of Paul [not including Hebrews], 1 Peter, 1 and 2 John, and the Revelation of John.[23] This list of New Testament books is strikingly similar to the "undisputed" list of twenty-two books of Origen. A minor difference concerns the status of 2 John, which Origen was willing to accept. In fact, it was accepted by Clement. But Origen knew it was "disputed." The major difference concerns the Pauline corpus. Hippolytus held to a thirteen letter Pauline corpus [excluding Hebrews]. According to Goodspeed, "Hippolytus' famous contemporary, Gaius of Rome, held the same view of the Pauline collection."[24] Hippolytus knew Hebrews but did not accept it as from Paul.[25] Goodspeed notes that a few years after the death of Hippolytus, Novatian of Rome engaged in a correspondence with Cyprian of Carthage, and that these letters and their other writings reflect much the same New Testament canon as that used by Hippolytus. In fact, Cyprian's New Testament was "precisely that of Hippolytus, except for 2 John."[26] Goodspeed observes, however, that 2 John is quoted by another North African writer of Cyprian's time, so that it "clearly belonged to the New Testament there."[27]

Then Goodspeed concludes his discussion of "The Age of Origen" in the following words:

> Thus, in the middle of the third century while eastern Christianity, under the influence of Origen was expanding [sic] the New Testament earlier sketched by Rome, the western churches still cherished its more primitive form.[28]

But is not this comprehensively to misconstrue the influence of Origen? Could not one as readily conclude from the evidence Goodspeed himself provides that Origen in fact was seeking to accommodate the Alexandrine tradition favoring a more inclusive and eclectic thirty-three or thirty-six book New Testament canon to the sterner Roman twenty-two book model?

There was one disputed book Origen would not agree to omit. That was Hebrews. But otherwise, there is striking agreement between Origen's "undisputed" twenty-two book canon and that of Hippolytus. That is the undeniable fact that needs to be explained, if at all possible.

Irenaeus was a teacher of Hippolytus, and it is of further significance that the New Testament canon of Irenaeus contains virtually the same twenty-two books included in the New Testament canon of Hippolytus. The major exception concerns the status of the Revelation of Peter which Irenaeus may have regarded as Scripture.

One thing is virtually certain. This more restricted New Testament canon did not originate in Alexandria. And Goodspeed's observation that Origen's visit to Rome cannot have been without influence upon the active mind of a young man still in his twenties is worth pondering. For it is natural to suppose that in emulating Hippolytus in writing commentaries on the Scriptures, Origen would also have been receptive to what Hippolytus (and, through Hippolytus, his teacher Irenaeus) had to say about which Christian books were accepted as "Scripture." This offers the best available explanation, though by no means a proven one, for the undeniable fact that the "undisputed" New Testament books of Origen are very close in number and name to the New Testament canon of Hippolytus and Irenaeus.[29]

A century later, a Eusebius could say, probably with considerable justice, that these "undisputed" New Testament books were accepted in almost all Churches. But at the beginning of the third century we cannot be sure that Clement's more inclusive, somewhat amorphous, and certainly less clearly defined New Testament canon was quite as representative in some parts of the Church, probably in Egypt, as the canon of Irenaeus and Hippolytus. How did that leaner Western canon become so normative for the Church at large if it was not helped along the way by the influential school of Alexandria under Origen's influence? And what investment did Origen have in the outcome of the discussion to which he contributed concerning the apostolic status of Hebrews? After all, there is literary evidence, which Origen himself acknowledged, indicating that Hebrews was not written by the apostle Paul. What could have been the grounds for Origen's position that Hebrews was to be accepted as having scriptural authority for Christians?

4. ORIGEN'S EXHORTATION TO MARTYRDOM

In the introduction to his book on Origen, Rowan Greer has observed:

> What can be written of the history of the Roman empire during Origen's lifetime is little more than a list of imperial murders, civil wars, and their disastrous consequences in social and economic life. Plague and famine, together with barbarous invasions, complete the picture.[30]

Greer notes the contrast between the anarchy of his times and the serenity of Origen's writings, and concludes that, though Origen was not concerned to address this anarchy directly, his visionary work was meant to have an impact upon the issues of his day. Specifically, Origen saw the Christian hope as "the catalyst that could rescue and transform what was best" in the Roman world.

> His theology was an attempt to translate the Gospel into a language intelligible to the pagan, especially the thoughtful and educated pagan. Side by side with the enterprise of translation went the martyr's conviction of the absolute and exclusive commitment demanded by the Christian religion. It can be argued that it was the success of Christianity in holding in tension such an absolute claim and the desire to become all things to all peoples that explains the rise of Christianity in the third century and its apparent triumph in the fourth.

Greer concludes: "However problematic a figure Origen was, it is difficult to deny him an important and even a central role in this development."[31]

We focus now on the central role of martyrdom in the thought of that person who more than any other pioneered the way for Christian theology in the third century. And we ask: What are the implications of Origen's concern with martyrdom for our understanding of the development of the New Testament canon in the third century?

The question of the canonical status of the Letter to the Hebrews is the single most important point at issue between Origen on the one hand, and Ignatius, Polycarp, Irenaeus, Hippolytus, Gaius of Rome, Cyprian, and Novatian of Rome on the other. Therefore, we will look at Origen's use of the Epistle to the Hebrews as a clue to what Origen thought about the New Testament canon, and the criteria that should be followed in deciding whether a particular book should be accepted as "apostolic."

Once the question of apostolicity arose as an explicit criterion in deciding what was to be canonical, there were basically two alternative paradigms to follow in those Churches which accepted both the Pauline corpus and the fourfold Gospel canon. One paradigm was found in Paul's letters, specifically in Galatians 1–2. This led to the view that the apostles were Peter, James, John and Paul, with Paul, the apostle to the Gentiles, as "the apostle."

The other alternative was to begin with the fourfold Gospel canon, where, in the Gospel according to Matthew, the twelve disciples whom Jesus called to be closely identified with him in mission are named as the twelve apostles (Mt 10:1–2). In this paradigm, Peter is clearly the leading apostle among "the twelve."

Wherever a Church had a New Testament canon in which both the Pauline corpus and the fourfold Gospel canon were perceived as parts of a comprehensive canon including the Scriptures Christians had inherited from their Jewish past, there was, of course, no possibility of sustaining one of these paradigms to the exclusion of the other. Nonetheless, these two basic paradigms are always potentially present ready to exert their influence. We see the influence of the "Pauline" paradigm becoming quite explicit when Clement says of his teachers that they preserved the tradition of "the blessed doctrine derived directly from the holy apostles, Peter, James, John and Paul."[32]

In this hermeneutical tradition, Paul becomes normative. With Clement this leads to what he calls "the canon of the Gospel,"[33] with Gospel defined first as the Gospel Paul and the other apostles preached. But, by extension through the use of "Gospel" in the opening formula that introduces the book known as the Gospel According to Mark, it becomes basically the text of the fourfold Gospel canon read so as to complement and supplement the "apostolic" text of the Pauline corpus. When the words, "Even if I give my body to be burned, but have not love, I am nothing," become a hermeneutical key for understanding Paul's teaching on Christian martyrdom, as they do for Clement, then the doctrine on "love of enemy" in the Sermon on the Mount becomes normative for understanding Jesus' teaching on martyrdom. The result is a highly individualistic version of Christianity congenial to middle-class existence, emphasizing the personal quest for moral and spiritual perfection perceived as "following the Gnostic life seeking the truth in word and deed."[34]

Origen has something quite different in mind. In his *Exhortation to Martyrdom,* he proceeds from the alternate paradigm. He goes to the mission discourse in Matthew. After all, it was the mission of the Church that was being threatened by the persecution in which his father was martyred. And now the persecution is aimed at the clergy who are responsible for the mission of the Church. He notes that it is not in Jesus' discourses to the multitudes (Sermon on the Mount, *et al.*) that he gives his prophecies on martyrdom, "but in those to the apostles." Then he cites the warning: "Beware of men; for they will deliver you up to councils, and flog you in their synagogues, and you will be dragged before governors and kings for my sake to bear testimony before them and the Gentiles. . . ."

In introducing the saying: "Do not fear those who kill the body but cannot kill the soul," Origen writes: "Also the following exhortation to martyrdom, found in Matthew, was spoken to no others but the twelve." Origen adds: "We, too, should hear it, since by hearing it we shall become brothers of the apostles who heard it and shall be numbered with the apostles." This reveals what Origen means by "apostolic." There is no necessary connection with the name "Matthew," nor even with the author of the text identified in the Church as the Gospel According to Matthew. These words addressed to the apostles have come true. The apostles did bear witness to the Gentiles. Christian martyrs had succeeded in enduring the destruction of their bodies. Origen and the Gentile Church are the fruit of that collective witness and that collective martyrdom. Origen believes that those who hear this exhortation to martyrdom and respond positively to it become brothers of the apostles who heard it originally.

If (a) it is only the martyr, who, for Origen, *truly* follows Christ and is in union with him, if (b) the disciple who takes up his cross and follows Jesus, for Origen, attains to an immediate knowledge of God whom he sees face to face, and if (c) this is a belief fundamental to Origen's ideas about the nature of the Church, then (d) it becomes clear why Origen could not agree to see Hebrews discounted simply on the grounds that it was not written by Paul. For, without Hebrews, Origen's belief about martyrdom which is so fundamental to his ideas about the nature of the Church would be missing an essential scriptural component, *which Origen knows to be "apostolic."*

Hebrews teaches that Jesus is the pioneer of faith. He leads his followers not just to the heavenly heights reached by Paul, who was caught up into the third heaven and heard things that cannot be told. His followers, if they do not shrink from what taking up their cross and following him means, will pass with him through the heavens (Hebrews 4:14). Once through the heavens, the followers of the pioneer of faith will be in the presence of the heavenly Father who will teach them. As friends who know by a real awareness these followers will comprehend "face to face."[35]

Absolutely crucial to Origen's peculiar form of mysticism is the doctrine that we come "face to face" with God who is our friend by taking up our cross and following Jesus. Equally essential to Origen's thought is the christological concept of Jesus as the pioneer of faith who "endured the cross, despising the shame, and, therefore, is seated at the right hand of God."[36] Origen makes explicit a logical connection between enduring the cross and being seated at the right hand of God, which is implicit in Hebrews. What is crucial for Origen's theology is this: Jesus is presently leading his followers to heaven. They can accompany him to heaven by mystically, and morally, sharing in his suffering. In this process, the followers of Jesus, like the pioneer of their faith, must endure to the end, realizing that "though they can kill the body, they cannot kill the soul." This is all made very explicit by Origen when he exhorts his lifelong friend and colleague, Ambrose, directly as follows:

> This is especially true of you, holy Ambrose ... if now, as it were, you go in procession bearing the cross of Jesus and following him when he brings you before governors and kings. His purpose is to go with you and give you your speech and wisdom ... and he is with you to show you the way to the paradise of God. . . .[37]

The imitation of Christ through martyrdom was essential to Origen's theology. That meant that he could readily agree to the leaner "undisputed" canon common to the Church in Alexandria and the Church at Rome. This was a canon which focused on martyrdom better than the less well-defined and more inclusive canon of his teacher Clement. Chadwick notes that Origen believed that "the particular value of martyrdom consisted in that the martyr knew himself to be in mystical union with his Lord in his passion."[38] Hebrews was very important in supplying essential scriptural support for this union of mysticism with martyrdom. It was Origen, through his use of Hebrews, who put an end in principle to Gnosticism by the simple doctrine that mystical knowledge of God comes not from disengaging from the world of pain and anarchy in order to lead a speculative existence or a life of contemplation. Mystical knowledge of God comes from the faithful disciple of Jesus taking up his or her cross and, in company with Jesus, following him as a Christian martyr.

5. SUMMARY CONCLUSIONS

It is clear that the essential New Testament canon which presently unites all Christians, both those who accept and those who do not accept Chalcedon, except for Hebrews, already was widely accepted by the time of Hippolytus. From Gaul in the West to Egypt in the East, the fourfold Gospel canon, Acts, a thirteen letter Pauline corpus, 1 Peter and 1 John were widely known, used, and held as authoritative.

Before turning to the topic of "Irenaeus and the Church of

Gaul," it will be helpful to dispel the notion that there was anything inevitable about the shape that the New Testament had achieved by the beginning of the third century, because a consideration of the different ways in which the New Testament canon *might* have developed proves that the eventual form that it *did* achieve was not a foregone conclusion. Harnack, for example, suggested that there were "seven different starting points of development that could have led to collections of works competing with the growing New Testament." Furthermore, he was able to show that "in part, these developments did not only start, but actually took definite form." Harnack refers to these seven starting points as seven "embryonic collections" and lists them as follows:[39]

(1) A collection of intertestamental and Christian prophetic-messianic or prophetic-hortatory books inserted in the Old Testament—thus, an expanded and corrected Old Testament. As examples, Harnack cites the *Book of Enoch,* the *Apocalypse of Ezra,* and the *Assumption of Moses.*

(2) A collection of (late Jewish and) Christian prophetic books standing independently side by side with the Old Testament. The Revelation of John, Harnack points out, was meant to stand side by side rather than inside the Old Testament.

(3) A simple collection of sayings of the Lord standing side by side with the Old Testament.

(4) A written Gospel, or a collection of several Gospels containing the history of the crucified and risen Lord, together with his teaching and commands, standing side by side with the Old Testament.

(5) A Gospel (or several) together with a more or less comprehensive collection of inspired Christian works of the most different character and graded prestige, standing side by side with the Old Testament. Harnack noted:

> The characteristic of this form is that although the idea of a collection of books of the "new covenant" in addition to the Gospel (the Gospels) has at last been realized, yet no clearness prevails as to the principle according to which further authoritative books are to be added to the Gospels. *The second half of the collection is still quite formless and is*

*therefore destitute of boundaries, nor is it closed against oth-
er works.* .... This is the condition of things presupposed by
Clement of Alexandria. . . .

(6) A systematized "teaching of the Lord" administered by the
"twelve apostles" of the character of the "apostolic canons, constitu-
tions, etc.," which also included "injunctions of the Lord," side by
side with the Old Testament and Gospel. We find the beginning of
such an embryonic collection in the *Didache,* i.e., "The Teaching of
the Lord by the Twelve Apostles."

(7) A book of the synthesis or concordance of prophecy and fulfillment in reference to Jesus Christ, the apostles, and the Church,
standing side by side with the Old Testament. Collections of messianic passages from the Old Testament were made by Jews. First attempts toward working out a comprehensive Christian synthesis of
messianic prophecies and fulfillment can be seen in those parts of the
Epistle of Barnabas, and the writings of Justin Martyr and Tertullian
that deal with such concordance.

To these seven embryonic canons of Harnack might be added:

(8) A collection of Paul's letters standing independently side by
side with the Old Testament. This presumably would have been the
situation in some Pauline Churches.

(9) A collection of Paul's letters together with a Gospel and a
systematic work showing the contradictions between the Scriptures
of the Jews and the Christian Scriptures. This was the form of Marcion's canon.

All of these nine collections of authoritative writings would
have been written. None of them would rule out the importance of
an oral tradition, particularly "words of the Lord." This oral tradition would have existed side by side with the Old Testament, plus
any one of these embryonic New Testaments. Only Marcion, who rejected the Old Testament, seems to have had a canon that was independent of such an oral tradition.

What follows from this is that the form the New Testament had
achieved by the end of the second century was by no means the only
form it conceivably could have assumed. In fact, that it achieved the
particular form it did cries out for explanation, especially in a day
when the public is becoming increasingly aware of the great diversity

of Christian Scriptures that prevailed in some parts of the Church, certainly in Egypt, and there certainly up into the fourth century.[40]

C. *Irenaeus and the Church of Gaul*

We have noted that Hippolytus was a student of Irenaeus, and that his New Testament canon agreed essentially with that of Irenaeus. In order to set the stage for understanding the influence of Irenaeus in forming the New Testament canon that emerged by the end of the second century, it will be helpful first to consider two documents preserved by Eusebius in his *Church History*.

1. THE FACTOR OF HERESY

Serapion, who became bishop in Antioch in A.D. 191 and died in A.D. 210, composed a book that was ostensibly addressed to the Church at Rhossus, about thirty miles from Antioch. But this book could have been used by anyone who needed to be warned about the "heretical" *Gospel of Peter.*

For our part, brethren, we receive both Peter and the other apostles as Christ, but the writings which falsely bear their names, we reject, as men of experience, knowing that such were not handed down to us. For I, myself, when I came among you, imagined that all of you clung to the true faith; and, without going through the Gospel put forward by them in the name of Peter, I said: If this is the only thing that seemingly causes captious feelings among you, let it be read. But since, from what has been told me, I have now learnt that their mind was lurking in some hole of heresy, I shall be diligent to come again to you; wherefore, brethren, expect me quickly. But we, brethren . . . with the assistance of those who studied this very Gospel, that is, by the successors of those who began it, whom we call Docetae (for most of the ideas belong to their teaching)—using [the material supplied] by them, were enabled to go through it and discover that most of it was in accordance with the true teaching of the Savior. But that some things were added. . . .[41]

This letter is important for showing how decisions regarding canon-icity were made. There was in the Church an awareness of the "true teaching of the Savior," as well as the "true faith." Apparently Bish-op Serapion was aided in making his "discoveries" about the *Gospel of Peter* by comparing it with older Gospels which had been "handed down" in the Church. When the *Gospel of Peter* was first written, it was permitted to be read, because, for the most part, it conformed to the true faith. But as time went on those who wrote the Gospel of Peter were succeeded by others who built on the docetic character of this Gospel and began to lead some of the faithful astray. Since these "false" teachers were able to justify their "docetic" views by appeal to the text of a Gospel which the good bishop had at first approved for being read, it was necessary for him to refute the false teaching in this Gospel and to explain the circumstances under which he once had unwittingly given it his approval.

The point to note is that *canon presupposes heresy.* At first there was no operational distinction that dictated the use of some Gospels and the rejection of others. Then came individuals and groups that used one or more of these Gospels to turn aside the faithful into het-erodox teachings. In order to combat these "heretics" it was neces-sary to discredit the apostolic authority of the Scriptures that justified their teaching. The concomitant effect of refuting the books of the "heretics" was to accord a special "canonical" status to those books that were accepted as "apostolic." Books which earlier had been perceived as Scriptures that are permitted to be read in the Churches are now perceived as books that, above and beyond this li-turgical function, have the added function of serving as a written canon or measure of the rule of faith. Previously they had been read in church because they were in line with the true faith. Now they are read in church for an additional reason. They are truly "apostolic," in contrast to the other Gospels which are falsely put forward as "ap-ostolic." They are in accord with the true teaching of the Savior, as the *Gospel of Peter* is not. As written expressions of that true teach-ing, they can be read in church when other Gospels cannot. They are now quite distinctive. They stand out from all the rejected Gospels. If one of them cannot be said to have been written by an apostle, then it can at least be associated with a disciple of an apostle. Gos-pels that have been handed down in the Church should be kept together and read and studied together. In this way the faithful will be mentally prepared to defend the true faith against all the dangerous new interpretations based on Gospels that had not been handed down from the earlier period.[42]

This indicates one way in which "heresy" was a formative factor in the shaping of the New Testament. For there was no single "heresy" that contributed to the forming of the New Testament; nor was there a single gathering of the bishops of the Churches to decide which books to accept and which to reject. There was rather a generation of practical-minded bishops like Serapion of Antioch who were disposed to be inclusive in their approach to ecclesiastical problems, had the courage to change their minds in the face of new evidence, and the scholarly resources to back up their theological and administrative decisions. Irenaeus was such a bishop.

But before we proceed to consider his formative contribution, it will be helpful to consider a second document from this same period. For this document makes it clear that in addition to "heresy" there was another formative factor at work, namely official persecution of Christians.

2. THE FACTOR OF PERSECUTION

Christians had suffered persecution at the hands of state officials at different times and at different places in the Roman empire long before Irenaeus.[43] But in about the year A.D. 178, under the emperor Antoninus Verus, persecution against Christians broke out anew in different parts of the world. We are able to form a vivid mental picture of the effect of this persecution of Christians in the province of Gaul where Irenaeus was a presbyter from a treatise preserved by Eusebius at the beginning of Book 5 of his *Ecclesiastical History*. This is a most remarkable document and of the greatest importance in illuminating the historical processes which contributed to the formation of the New Testament canon.

After some introductory comments, Eusebius justifies his inclusion of this document with the following observation:

Other writers of historical works have confined themselves
to giving accounts of victories won in wars, and conquests

of enemies, of the exploits of generals and brave deeds of soldiers, men stained with the blood of countless numbers of those they killed for the sake of children and fatherland and other possessions; but our history of those who order their lives according to God will inscribe on everlasting monuments the record of most peaceful wars waged for the very peace of the soul, and of those who in such wars have been valiant for truth, rather than for fatherland, and for piety rather than for the dearest members of their families; our history will proclaim for everlasting remembrance the struggles of the champions of piety and their deeds of bravery and endurance, conquests of demons and victories over unseen adversaries, and crowns gained when all was accomplished.[44]

The Christians, according to this perception, were engaged in a peaceful war contending valiantly for truth, and in this war the Christian martyrs were champions of God. Their deeds of bravery and endurance brought victory over devils and invisible adversaries. As we follow the text of the letter cited by Eusebius, we are looking especially for what we can learn about the import of New Testament Scriptures for this peaceful war against devils and invisible adversaries. What role did Christian Scripture play in bringing the Roman imperial authority to bay?

Eusebius continues:

Gaul was the country in which was prepared the stage for these events. Its capital cities . . . were Lyons and Vienne, through both of which passes the Rhone River, flowing in an ample stream through the entire country. Now, the most illustrious of the Churches of this country circulated an account of their martyrs among the Churches of Asia and Phrygia. . . . I will quote their words: "The servants of Christ sojourning in Vienne and Lyons in Gaul to the brethren in Asia and Phrygia, who have the same faith and hope of redemption as you. Peace and grace and glory from God, the Father and Christ Jesus our Lord."

Then, after other prefatory remarks, they begin their account in the following way: "The greatness of the persecution here, and the terrible rage of the heathen against the saints, and all that the blessed martyrs endured is beyond the power of pen to narrate accurately. For with all his might the adversary attacked us, giving us a foretaste of his coming which is shortly to be. He tried everything, training and exercising his adherents to act against the servants of God, to the end that we were not merely excluded from houses and baths and market place, but they even forbade any of us to be seen at all in any place whatsoever. But, against them, the grace of God did act as our captain; he rescued the weak, and set up over against the foe steadfast pillars able by their endurance to draw upon themselves the whole attack of the evil one.   *

According to 1 Tim 3:15, the Church is the pillar and bulwark of truth. And in Gal 2:9, the apostles Peter, James, and John (martyrs all) are referred to as pillars of the Church. In this letter the imagery of the warrior hero who drew all the spears of the enemy line into his own body—making himself a living sacrifice so that victory could be achieved by those who rushed through the resulting gap in the opposing line—has been combined with scriptural imagery to forge a powerful new image of the Christian martyr, the champion of truth.[45] Through the sacrifices of such martyrs victory will come if only they can endure the attack of the evil one. They must expect the most demonic form of torture and destruction to fall upon them. These dedicated men and women will join together to forge an invincible defense of peace and concord and love. They will acknowledge no race and answer to no name but "Christian." The letter continues:

These indomitable pillars closed ranks, enduring every kind of reproach and punishment; yea, regarding their many trials as virtually nothing, they hastened to Christ and did indeed prove *that the sufferings of this present time are not worthy to be compared with the glory which shall be revealed to us.*

This citation from the apostle Paul (Rom 8:18), though not identified as such, would not have gone unnoticed in Asia and Phrygia, since Paul's letters had long since been collected and were circulating throughout the Church. These were the words of one who had suffered imprisonments and countless beatings and was often near death. He had been stoned, shipwrecked, and placed in all kinds of danger, and he spent many a sleepless night in hunger and thirst, often without food, in cold and exposure (2 Cor 11:23–27). Paul was a man "in Christ," who had exhorted others to be imitators of him as he was of Christ, and who, like his crucified Savior, had died a martyr at the hands of the Roman authorities. This affords a glimpse of something very important. *The New Testament* (where the Gospels of Christ are united with the letters of Paul by the Acts of the Apostles) *is the book of the covenant of Christ* to all who stand in the martyrological tradition of Jesus and the apostles—above all, the apostles Peter and Paul who were believed to have made their final witness and received their crown of martyrdom in the very seat of the "evil one's" authority.

3. IRENAEUS AND THE MARTYRS OF GAUL

Later, some of the surviving Christian martyrs in Gaul gave Irenaeus a letter of commendation and addressed it to the bishop of Rome:

> Once more and always, Father Eleutherus, we greet you prayerfully in God. We have asked our brother and comrade Irenaeus to bring this letter to you and we beseech you to hold him in esteem, for he is a zealot *for the covenant of Christ.* . . .[46]

As we shall see, Irenaeus did not speak and write only for himself. He went as a presbyter to Rome with the backing of the martyrs of Gaul. He returned to Gaul to become a spokesman for the whole Church, and, after the martyrdom of his bishop, he was made bishop of Lyons. Irenaeus never forgot that he was the martyrs' bishop, and his New Testament embraced the Scriptures of the martyrs. The Gospels reminded all Christians of the martyrdom of Jesus; the epistles reminded them of the martyrdom of the apostles; Acts reminded them of the martyrdom of Stephen; the Revelation of John reminded them of the martyrdom of the saints. Virtually the whole of what Irenaeus championed as New Testament Scripture reminded the Church of the central role of martyrdom in the life of God's people.

Gospels without the passion of Jesus Christ, like the infancy Gospels or the Gospel of Thomas, were of little interest to Christian martyrs. Moreover, Docetic Gospels which suggested that Jesus Christ had not really suffered on the cross or had not suffered the death of crucifixion, like the Gospel of Peter, had to be repudiated as subversive among the ranks of those engaged in the "peaceful" life and death struggle with the "evil one."

In this way, the factor of "heresy" is joined with the factor of persecution. The two are not to be thought of as entirely separate factors. In the processes forming the New Testament, these two factors are intimately interrelated. It is no accident that the most comprehensive and influential tract against "heresy" of the early Church was written by the bishop of Lyons, brother and comrade of the martyrs of Gaul.

During the persecution in Gaul, Christians had been accused of the most inflammatory charges—of eating their children and of incest. As such rumors spread, the whole populace was infuriated, and even those who had hitherto behaved with moderation, on the grounds of kinship, now turned against their own friends and relatives who had become Christians and cooperated with their persecutors. We resume the account in the letter from the martyrs of Gaul at this point:

> The entire fury of the mob and of the governor and of the soldiers was raised beyond measure against Sanctus, the deacon from Vienne ... and against Blandina, through whom Christ showed that things which are mean and obscure and contemptible in the eyes of men are accounted worthy of great glory with God because of the love toward him, a love which showed itself in power and did not boast of itself in appearance. For while we were all afraid, and her human mistress, who herself was also a combatant in the ranks of the martyrs, was in distress lest she should not

be able, through the weakness of her body, to be bold enough to make confession, Blandina was filled with such power that she was released and rescued from those who took turns in torturing her in every way from morning until evening, and they themselves admitted that they were beaten, for they marveled that she still remained alive, since her whole body was mangled and filled with gaping wounds, and they testified that any one of these tortures was sufficient to destroy life, even when these tortures had not been multiplied and intensified. But the blessed woman, like a noble champion, kept gaining in vigor in her confession, and found comfort and refreshment and freedom from pain from what was done to her by repeating: "I am a Christian woman and no foul thing happens amongst us."

Sanctus also nobly endured with surpassing courage all the torment that human hands could inflict. For, though the wicked hoped through persistence and the rigor of his tortures to wring from him some admission of wrong-doing, he resisted them with such firmness that he would not even state his own name, or the race or the city whence he came, nor whether he was slave or free. To all questions, he answered in Latin, "I am a Christian." This he repeated for name and city and race and for everything else, and no other word did the heathen hear from him.[47]

What eloquent testimony to the fact that Christian faith had the power to give people a new identity! They were no longer Romans, Phrygians, or Jews, but Christians, members of a new covenant people. Each person was a new creation, with a new superhuman and almost divine capacity to withstand the demonic wiles of the "evil one." This was without doubt a powerful witness to the fact that in Christ there was neither male nor female, Jew nor Gentile, slave nor free.

As the letter continues, it is related that the authorities even went so far as to suspend the gladiatorial contests and substituted the spectacle of hanging Blandina on a stake, offering her as a prey to the wild beasts that were let in.

She seemed to be hanging in the shape of a cross, and by her continuous prayer, she greatly encouraged those around her who were contending. For, in their torment, they beheld with their outward eyes, in the form of their sister, him who was crucified for them. The effect was to persuade those who believe on him that all who suffer for the glory of Christ have eternal fellowship with the living God. And, as none of the wild beasts then touched her, she was taken down from the stake and cast again into prison. . . .

Here again, there is every reason to think that the Gospels with the dramatic foreshadowing of the death of Christ and the events of Passion Week followed by the Resurrection stories, as well as Paul's letters with their emphasis upon the cross of Christ, were a formative influence upon the minds of those who would record an event like this in such terms, if not, indeed, upon the minds of those who actually withstood such tortures.

The effect of this faithfulness was to move many who had at first given in to their persecutors to change their minds and decide that they too wanted to join their brothers and sisters in making their confession. The governor accordingly examined these persons again, sending all who confessed their faith as Christians to their death.

After copying out a great deal more of the letter, Eusebius pauses to comment:

Such things happened to the Churches of Christ under the emperor mentioned, and from these things it is possible to form a reasonable conclusion as to what was done in other provinces. It is worthwhile to add other statements from the same document in which the gentleness and the kindness of the martyrs already mentioned have been set down in these very words: "And they carried so far their zeal and imitation of Christ . . . that for all their glory, and though they had testified not once or twice, but many times, and had been taken back from the beasts and were covered with burns and scars and wounds, they neither proclaimed themselves as martyrs, nor allowed us to address them by this title; nay, they severely rebuked any one of us who so styled them in letter or conversation. For they gladly conceded the title of martyr to Christ, the faithful and true martyr. . . .They conceded that those who had given their lives in faithful witness were martyrs, but that those who did not actually depart this life are not—they are only "confessors."

Eusebius writes that a little farther on in the letter it is said:

They humbled themselves under the mighty hand, by which they are not greatly exalted. At that time, they made defense for all men; against none did they bring accusation; they released all and bound none; and they prayed for those who had inflicted torture, even as did Stephen, the perfect martyr: *Lord, lay not this sin to their charge.* And if Stephen prayed thus for those who were stoning him, how much more (should we pray) for the brethren (who have lapsed).[48]

This is the earliest clear example of the influence of the Book of Acts in the life of the Church. The example of Stephen as the perfect martyr, taken together with the imprisonments of the apostles and other hardships inflicted on the first Christians recounted in Acts, as well as such sayings as "we must obey God, not men," apparently turned the Book of Acts into a Scripture of special interest and importance to Churches under persecution. Eusebius skips over other parts of the letter and then picks up the narrative again:

For their greatest contest with the beast (i.e., the "evil one"), through the genuineness of their love, was this: that the beast should be choked into throwing up alive those whom he had at first thought to have swallowed down (i.e., they sought the redemption of their Christian brothers and sisters who had denied the faith). For, they did not boast over the fallen, but from their own abundance supplied with a mother's love those that needed. And, shedding many tears for them to the Father, they prayed for life, and he gave it to them, and they divided it among their neighbors, and then departed to God, having in all things carried off the victory. They ever loved peace; peace they commended to us; and with peace they departed to God; for their mother (the Church) they left behind no sorrow, and for the brethren no strife and war, but rather glory, peace, concord and love.[49]

Eusebius, wanting to emphasize the forgiving attitude of these martyrs toward those who had lapsed, in contrast to the recalcitrant attitude of some of his own contemporaries like the Donatists and Novatians, adds:

This record of the affection of those blessed ones for the brethren who had fallen may profitably be set forth, in view of the inhuman and merciless temper displayed by those who afterward behaved so harshly toward members of Christ.[50]

4. A MARTYRS' CANON OF SCRIPTURE

The reference to the imagery of the "beast" of the Revelation of John is obvious. But this Scripture is not by itself a norm for the martyrs of Gaul. In the background, in addition to the conciliatory words of "the perfect martyr," Stephen, there are the norming words of the martyred apostle Paul: "If we give our bodies to be burned and have not love, we are nothing." And, above all, there looms the magisterial norm of the example of "the faithful and true martyr" who was recorded to have prayed: *Father, forgive them, for they know not what they do,* and who taught his disciples to seek out the lost and to forgive the brothers who sin against them *not seven times, but seventy times seven.*

We see emerging not simply a martyrs' canon of Christian Scripture. We see emerging a *particular* martyrs' canon.[51] This canon featured the Revelation of John, the Acts of the Apostles, and the Epistles of Paul, all read in the light of the fourfold Gospel canon. Martyrs who live by this norm will not only risk their lives for the sake of Christ and for the sake of his Gospel, but they will refuse to condemn those who, under persecution, became apostates and will in all matters strive to achieve concord and peace as they seek to reunite the family of God. There is a remarkable overall kinship between the text of this letter and the New Testament. There are over seventy possible allusions to the books of the New Testament noted in this letter in the Lawlor-Oulton edition of Eusebius' *Ecclesiastical History*. There are seventeen possible cross-references to the Gospels, twelve for the Acts of the Apostles, thirty for the Pauline Epistles, including the Pastorals, one for Hebrews, two for 1 John, three for 1 Peter, four for 2 Peter, and five for Revelation. The remaining references are: three for the Psalms, two for Isaiah, one for Ezekiel, one for 2 Maccabees, two for Daniel, and two for Ignatius.

It is striking that the only New Testament books neither cited nor alluded to in this remarkable document are James, Jude, 2 and 3 John, Titus and Philemon. Except for Titus and Philemon, which would be included in the Pauline corpus, the New Testament books either not alluded to or not cited in this document are also not included in the New Testament canon of Irenaeus, nor the "undisputed" category of New Testament writings of Origen.

Or, to state the matter positively, the New Testament books which are not in dispute in the Church after Irenaeus are almost without exception books which had special meaning for certain known Churches that had experienced persecution. Furthermore, the very close relationship between the New Testament books cited or alluded to in this document (coming from the Rhone Valley) and the New Testament Scriptures acknowledged by Irenaeus (bishop of the Church in the Rhone Valley) strengthens our contention that the New Testament canon of Irenaeus has been profoundly influenced by the factor of persecution and martyrdom. Irenaeus makes no mention of 2 Peter, whereas it may be alluded to four times in this document. This document does not allude to the *Shepherd of Hermas* which Irenaeus cited as Scripture. But with these exceptions, the correspondence between the New Testament books alluded to in this letter and the canon of Irenaeus is truly striking.

One could and should note, of course, that all New Testament books cited and alluded to in this document existed long before the persecution that broke out in A.D. 178. So, we have not necessarily

answered the question "Whence came the New Testament?" by identifying and clarifying the importance of Christian martyrdom. We
have only put our finger on an important reason why this set of
Christian writings, rather than some other, emerged as the canon of
the Church. This reason is persecution. It is only one reason, but it is
a major one. The New Testament of the Church serves the needs of
Christians under persecution in a most adequate and inspiring manner. It does not encourage blind fanaticism, nor does it sustain self-
righteousness. It has the power, however, to nourish and guide not
only Christian saints but Christian confessors and martyrs, as well.
For Churches having experienced persecution, these Scriptures
would be known as sacrosanct books—books of God, books that
make the difference between life and death. These are books that
Churches will cherish and hand down with love and affection. They
will be holy books—consecrated by the blood of martyrs.

5. SOME ECCLESIASTICAL CONSEQUENCES OF MARTYRDOM

Following his extensive quotations from this letter to the Christians in Asia and Phrygia, Eusebius records further information
about the activities of the martyrs from Gaul:

> Just at that time, the party of Montanus and Alcibiades
> and Theodotus, in the region of Phrygia, were winning a
> widespread reputation for prophecy (for the many other
> wonderful works of the grace of God which were still being
> wrought up to that time in various Churches caused a
> widespread belief that they also were prophets). And when
> dissension arose about Montanus and the others, the breth-
> ren in Gaul again formulated their own judgment, pious
> and most orthodox, concerning them, subjoining various
> letters from the martyrs who had been consecrated among
> them, which letters they had composed, while they were
> still in prison, for the brethren in Asia and Phrygia, and
> also for Eleutherus, who was then bishop of the Romans,
> negotiating for the sake of the peace of the Churches.[52]

It is clear that the Church in Gaul, during the persecution, had been an underground Church. Christians in prison for the sake of the Gospel, like the apostle Paul before them, and countless Christian prisoners since, redeemed the time by writing letters. And some of these letters were to be carried great distances, even greater distances than any known letter that Paul had sent. It is clear that the authorities in Gaul had imprisoned not simply some zealous Christians, eager to win the crown of martyrdom, but leaders of the Church who had a vision of its organic and visible unity. Other Christians needed to be informed about what was happening to the Church of God in the Rhone Valley. And, no doubt, the Christians in that remote province needed outside contacts with Christians in other parts of the empire. Thus we may be confident that there grew up an informational and inspirational network of correspondence as well as oral communication between Christians who identified with one another and provided mutual support whenever persecution broke out in different parts of the empire. The weak links in the chain of mutually supporting Churches that united Christians within the empire would have been those Churches under Gnostic influence. In these Churches, as Elaine Pagels has shown, there was a tendency to question the value of martyrdom.[53]

These Churches found in the Christian Scriptures, especially in the letters of Paul, grounds for a quite different spirituality, a spirituality that did not move Christians into positions of opposition to the imperial authorities, and thus did not pose the same need for mutual support from Christians in other parts of the empire, nor for disciplined episcopal leadership and inter-regional consultation.[54] Outstanding men like Valentinus might journey to Rome, but their goal was to propagate their new doctrine in the capital of the empire, not to consult with the bishop of Rome to find that common ground on which all Christians could unite in their defense of the faith against an opposition from the state that threatened the extinction of apostolic Christian belief and practice.

The persecution that the Church in Gaul had gone through had been shared by other Churches in other parts of the empire. Irenaeus knew all about this and understood very well what was at stake. The blood of the martyrs, beginning with Jesus, was the seed of the Church. This Church was now threatened by a seemingly uncontrolled plethora of theological and exegetical speculation which sapped the strength of the Church in its resistance against the wiles of the "evil one." It was to do battle against this immediate and long-term threat that Irenaeus undertook to write his *magnum opus.*

6. IRENAEUS: *AGAINST HERESIES*

Irenaeus began his work *Against Heresies* with an analysis of the works of the Valentinians, and especially their use of the Scriptures (1.1–9). He then took up the subject of the Church and asserted that the faith once given to the apostles had been handed down through the Church until his own time. He intended neither to add to nor to diminish that faith (1.10). Irenaeus then returned to his attack. Considering the views of numerous Christian writers, he refuted their use of the Scriptures which had been handed down in the Church, and discredited their new "spurious" Scriptures (1.11–31). In Book 2, Irenaeus continued his refutation in great detail and claimed to have been able to trace the origin of all heresy to its father Simon.

In Book 3, Irenaeus took up the Christian Scriptures and strengthened his case against those he opposed by building an historical and scriptural defense of what he understood to be the true and apostolic faith. In chapter 1, he wrote:

We have learned from none others the plan of our salvation than from those through whom the Gospel has come down to us, which they did at one time proclaim in public, and, at a later period, by the will of God, handed down to us in the Scriptures, to be the ground and pillar of our faith.

Irenaeus drew upon the Acts of the Apostles for the story of Pentecost and the apostolic preaching mission. Then came his famous tradition concerning the authorship and provenance of Matthew, Mark, Luke, and John (3.1). As to the "heretics' " point that truth concerning the faith was not delivered by means of written documents, but *viva voce,* Irenaeus responded with the *viva vox* of the tradition that originated with the apostles! If the apostles had known hidden mysteries, which they were in the habit of imparting to "the perfect," apart from and privately to the other Christians, they would certainly have delivered them to those into whose hands they were committing the churches they had founded.

Irenaeus argues that since we can trace the succession of bishops in the major Churches from the apostles to the present, we can be sure that, in the faith handed down to us in these Churches, we have the true apostolic faith. This is confirmed by the fact that the faith adhered to in all these Churches is the same. We can go to the heart of the matter by taking up the tradition as it has come down to us from the apostles of the very great, the very ancient, and universally known Church founded and organized at Rome by the two most glorious apostles, Peter and Paul, who, having founded and built up the church in Rome, committed the office of bishop into the hands of Linus. From Linus until now, it is possible to name in succession all twelve bishops of the Church in Rome. With Valentinus, Marcion, and the other heretics, the situation is quite different. None of them can trace his authority back through any episcopal line to an apostle. Each claims that he has the authority to say what the truth is by interpreting the Scriptures according to some private understanding or some secret revelation. But these Scriptures, when rightly read, only serve to refute the views of these heretics and confirm the apostolic faith that is taught in all the Churches (3.2–25).

This, in brief compass, is Irenaeus' fundamental line of reasoning. Chapter 18 is of special interest because there Irenaeus treats the subject of persecution and martyrdom and we are provided the opportunity to see how, in fact, he viewed the matter. He begins with a series of passages from the letters of Paul to establish the point that Jesus Christ truly lived, suffered, and died. Rom 14:9, "For to this end Christ both lived and died, and revived, that he might rule over the living and the dead." 1 Cor 1:23, "But we preach Christ Jesus crucified." 1 Cor 15:3–4, "For, I delivered unto you, first of all, that Christ died for our sins. . . ." Irenaeus concludes, "It is plain, then, that Paul knew no other Christ besides him alone who both suffered, and was buried, and rose again, who was also born, and whom he speaks of as human. . . . And everywhere, when referring to the passion of our Lord, and to his human nature, and his subjection to death, he employs the name of Christ, as in that passage: 'Destroy not him with thy meat for whom Christ died.' "

Irenaeus then, without referring to the Gospels by name, turns to Matthew and Luke and argues as follows: After Jesus asked his disciples "Who do men say that I am?" it is said that "he began to show to his disciples, now that he must go to Jerusalem and suffer many things of the priests, and be rejected, and crucified, and rise again on the third day." Jesus went on to say, "If any man will come after me, let him deny himself, and take up his cross, and follow me. For whosoever will save his life shall lose it; and whosoever will lose it for my sake shall save it." Irenaeus concludes this stage of his argument with these words: "For these things Christ spoke openly, he being himself the Savior of those who should be delivered over to death for their confession of him, and lose their lives."

Next, Irenaeus takes up the view that Christ was not to suffer and therefore left the body of Jesus on the cross, and asks rhetorically, "Why then did he exhort his disciples to take up the cross and follow him?" He notes that Jesus said to the Jews: "Behold, I send you prophets, and wise men, and scribes: and some of them you shall kill and crucify." This implies, reasons Irenaeus, that Jesus expected his disciples to suffer for his sake. To his disciples Jesus said: "Ye shall stand before governors and kings for my sake; and they shall scourge some of you, and slay you, and persecute you from city to city." Jesus knew that his disciples would suffer persecution and would be killed and he did not speak of any other cross than of the suffering which he himself should first undergo, and his disciples afterward. For this reason, he said: "Fear not them which kill the body, but are not able to kill the soul; but rather fear him who is able to send both soul and body into hell," thus exhorting them to hold fast to those professions of faith which they had made concerning him.

> For he promised to confess before his Father those who should confess his name before men; but declared that he would deny those who should deny him, and would be ashamed of those who should be ashamed to confess him. And, although these things are so, some of these men have proceeded to such a degree of temerity, that they even pour contempt upon martyrs, and vituperate those who are slain on account of the confession of the Lord, and who suffer all

things predicted by the Lord, and who in this respect strive to follow the footprints of the Lord's passion, having become martyrs of the suffering One. . . . And from this fact, that he exclaimed upon the cross, "Father, forgive them, for they know not what they do," the long-suffering patience, compassion, and goodness of Christ are exhibited, since he both suffered, and did himself exculpate those who had maltreated him. For the Word of God, who said to us "Love your enemies, and pray for those that hate you," himself did this very thing upon the cross, loving the human race to such a degree that he even prayed for those putting him to death.

Irenaeus concludes that, assuming for the sake of argument that there were two Christs, one who suffered on the cross and another who flew away, the truly good one would have been the "one who, in the midst of his own wounds and stripes and other cruelties inflicted upon him, was beneficent, and unmindful of the wrongs perpetrated upon him," rather than "he who flew away, and sustained neither injury nor insult." As for the similar view that Jesus only "seemed" to suffer, Irenaeus has this to say:

If he did not truly suffer, no thanks to him, since there was no suffering at all; and when we shall actually begin to suffer, he will seem as leading us astray, exhorting us to endure buffeting, and to turn the other cheek, if he did not himself before us in reality suffer the same; and as he misled them by seeming to them to be suffering when he was not, so does he also mislead us, by exhorting us to endure what he did not endure himself.

7. SUMMARY CONCLUSIONS

In Irenaeus' theological system the Scriptures function in two ways. They have been handed down in the Church and witness to the faith of the apostles. But they also provide an excellent basis for refuting "heretics," because it can be shown by appeal to these Scriptures that the "heretics' " views are mistaken.

Just as Justin Martyr in an earlier period disproved the views of the Jews by appeal to the Scriptures of the Jews, so Irenaeus, as the apologist for the Catholic faith, disproved the views of the "heretics" by appeal to the Scriptures of the "heretics." And just as in the dispute with the Jews it became necessary to distinguish the books each side would accept as Scripture, so in the dispute with the "heretics" it became necessary to distinguish the books that each would accept as Scripture. From the side of Irenaeus, this required discrediting the "new" Scriptures of the "heretics." *The Gospel of Peter* and Marcion's Gospel are but examples of new Scriptures that needed to be discredited. With Irenaeus, Matthew, Mark, Luke, and John have a new status. These Scriptures not only bear witness to the Gospel, or the rule of faith, that was given to the apostles by Christ, but they can also serve as a written canon or norm or measure of the faith by which it is possible to disprove the views of the "heretics" and thus to prove that their new Gospels are not reliable.

Irenaeus, more than any other Church Father, helped the Church to sort out its thinking about its Scriptures. After Irenaeus, there was never again any serious thought given to rejecting the Old Testament. The fourfold Gospel canon of Matthew, Mark, Luke and John, thereafter, was firmly placed at the head of all lists of New Testament books. Acts, which had been used by the martyrs of Gaul, at the hands of Irenaeus emerged for the first time as an important Scripture of the Church.

Marcion and Valentinus had made much of the apostle Paul. Irenaeus embraced Paul fully, but insisted that there were other apostles. Peter was of special importance. For the teaching of the apostle Peter, Irenaeus relied primarily on the speeches of Peter in the Acts of the Apostles. For this reason, Acts was indispensable for Irenaeus. Moreover, Irenaeus used the Acts of the Apostles, along with Paul's letters (including the Pastorals), for his sources for the teaching of Paul. Formally speaking, Acts united the fourfold Gospel canon with the Epistles of Paul, and Paul with those disciples of Jesus who had been apostles before him. Finally, Irenaeus, with the help of John's Apocalypse, "reaches right to the consummation of history in the millennial kingdom."[55]

With Irenaeus, the Church had all the essential parts of what came to be its New Testament canon. There was the fourfold Gospel, Acts of the Apostles, letters of apostles, and the Revelation of John. Moreover, Irenaeus articulated the rationale for understanding the Scriptures of the Old and New Testaments as parts of one comprehensive and coherent canon.

If we will more fully appreciate Irenaeus' contribution, we will not only consider the importance of persecution and "heresy" in his own immediate background. We will also consider what had happened in Rome and other parts of the Church during the two previous generations. This has primarily to do with the formation of the fourfold Gospel canon and the earlier collection and publication of Paul's letters, and with the need of the Church to find some way to unite these two collections into a more inclusive canon of Scripture that would support and guide the Church in fulfilling its mission to preach the Gospel and make disciples of all the Gentiles. This carries us back into the archaic phase of canon making where the New Testament that eventually emerged in the Church had its beginning.[56]

D. *The Archaic Phase: The Beginning of the Canon*

1. THE FUNDAMENTALS OF THE CHRISTIAN CANON

What are the underlying factors which led to the developed textual appearance of the New Testament? We ask not about the deeper and wider theological matters like faith in the God of Israel and belief in the saving benefits of the death of Jesus Christ. We focus rather on the earliest relation of "Scripture" to these primal matters of faith and belief.

a. Scripture and Spirit

The Scriptures of Israel which Jesus and his disciples read witnessed to the reality of the Spirit of the Lord working in history and in creation. In turn, the Spirit of the Lord was felt to be in Jesus and in his followers and that Spirit gave them the authority to interpret the Scriptures and, when necessary, to supersede them with new revelation. Some of these Christians were inspired by the Spirit to speak in the name of the Lord. Thus, the sayings of Jesus remembered from his earthly ministry were augmented by new sayings from Christian prophets who, in the Spirit of Jesus and in his name, gave the Church new life-giving sayings. Some of these were also remembered and handed down with the other remembered sayings as "words of the Lord."[57]

This developing corpus of oral tradition of sayings of the Lord was handed down in different Churches in ways that reflected their different interests and needs. There never was one single uniform and set body of oral tradition that was handed down unaltered in all Churches. However, evidence provided by the Gospels, where much of this oral tradition has been preserved in written form, indicates that along with variation there was an abiding consistency in the intention of these remembered "words of the Lord." As new situations developed in the Church, which required new sayings of the Lord, there was a norm by which the Church could distinguish between true prophets and false prophets. The Church which remembered Jesus was in a position to recognize when prophets who were in the spirit of the Lord were speaking in accord with the Jesus they remembered or not. When the words spoken were not in accord with the Spirit of Jesus, as he was remembered and known in the Church, they were forgotten, if not rejected on the spot, and thus not handed down as "words of the Lord."

The words of the Lord that were remembered best were those that were most often recalled to memory and repeated. In this way selection resulted according to the differing needs of the respective Churches. These differing needs also resulted in different words being spoken by Christian prophets in different Churches. Thus, without doubt the oral tradition developed in different ways. However, the same spirit and some of the essential qualities of the original memory of Jesus must have remained alive in many Churches. Otherwise it would be impossible to explain, granting all the diversity that was inevitably and necessarily introduced, how these Churches could recognize each other as one Church adhering to a faith in the same Christ, even after several generations had passed and quite new social and cultural differences had grown up to distinguish these Churches from one another. This conclusion does not discount the very real importance of historical continuity in Church leadership. But it does recognize that such continuity in and of itself could not guarantee the unity that diverse Christian communities recognize when they come to know one another even after long periods of separation.

Until such time as the need arose for these words of the Lord to be written down, the only Scriptures in the Churches were those that, from the beginning, had been recognized as such by Jesus and his disciples. The first evident need for writing down the words of the Lord may have been in connection with the need for the oral tradition to be translated in a reliable way into languages other than that spoken by Jesus, or other than that spoken by Christian prophets speaking in the spirit and name of Jesus.

Once these words of Jesus, written in Greek, were incorporated into Greek Gospels, the Gospels, in turn, became Scripture for Greek-speaking Christians, *since they contained written "words of the Lord."* The distinction, however, between the written words of the Lord contained in the Gospels and the written narrative accounts of the evangelists was well understood in the early Church. As late as Irenaeus, the "words of the Lord" are cited from the Gospels without acknowledging that that is where they may be found. At the same time, "words of the Lord" (or sayings) are cited by Church Fathers that are not in any Gospel. This further confirms the fact that these words had a separate existence in the Church that was distinguishable from their presence in one or another of the Gospels.[58]

We are not to think that there was some comprehensive project of rendering the oral tradition of the words of Jesus into Greek on some large and uniform scale. Missionary work of this kind may sometimes be so envisioned by a dreamer. But the hard realities are different. The work proceeds as it is prompted by the spirit. Missional priorities vary from time to time in the same place, and from place to place at the same time. The work progresses in a practical way—first this saying and then that, first these sayings and then those. Translations of certain sayings into Greek made elsewhere and brought to Jerusalem would be valuable assets in the process. The changing situations on the mission field must be borne in mind. So it has always been in the missionary translation work of the Church.

The earliest beginnings of a distinctively Christian canon would have been the writings of the prophets and other Jewish Scriptures, handed on by Jesus and his disciples, plus the "words of the Lord," oral and written. Once the Gospels were written, they would have been regarded as books to be added to the already existing Scriptures because they, too, like the Scriptures inherited from Judaism, contained "words of the Lord."

It is important to realize that as far as the first Christians were concerned, there was no need for a new set of Scriptures. From the beginning in the Church, the books of Moses, the books of the prophets and the other Jewish Scriptures were read christologically, i.e., on the premise that the voice of the Lord could be heard in all Scripture addressing itself to the messianic presence of the reader. So, these Scriptures were no less Christian than anything written by a Christian.

Not everyone who read these Scriptures agreed with the way they were understood by Christians. It is clear, therefore, that something besides the Scriptures themselves was at work among the Christians that enabled them to read these writings as they did. This is the Gospel faith that originated with Jesus and his disciples, and which, following his death and resurrection, developed into what Paul could refer to as "the faith" (Gal 1:23), but which he generally calls "the Gospel." This "faith-Gospel" preceded all distinctively Christian writings. It did not, of course, precede in time the first Christian Scripture, i.e., the part of our present Christian Bible referred to as the Old Testament. This "faith-Gospel" also was the source of the Christian's interpretation of the writings of Moses, the prophets and the other Jewish Scriptures. There was, however, a reciprocal relationship between these Scriptures and the "faith-Gospel" that precludes speaking in strict terms of priority. It is really impossible to know, on the one hand, to what extent the Gospel Jesus preached was a product of his reflection on the meaning of the Scriptures, and, on the other, to what extent it was a special revelation. The two appear to have been inextricably bound up together.

The point to recognize is this: In the beginning the "words of the Lord" functioned as a living oral canon of the "faith-Gospel." All else was normed by this "faith-Gospel" canon, including "Moses and the prophets." To the books of Moses, the prophets and other Jewish Scriptures, *read christologically*, were added the written Gospels: this was the first and earliest beginning of a "form" which developed eventually into the Christian canon, its chief beginning.

b. Scripture and Apostolic Presence
(1) *Paul and the Scriptures*

Paul, like the other apostles, accepted the same Jewish Scriptures that had been received and handed on by Jesus and his disciples. However, as the apostle to the Gentiles, when he was working in Greek-speaking circles, Paul no doubt accepted these Scriptures as they had developed in the Greek-speaking Jewish diaspora.

In carrying out his mission to the Gentiles, Paul found scriptural authority for his special mission, above all, in the story of Abraham and in the Book of Isaiah.

In his Letter to the Romans, there is a central section (9:19–10:21) in which he provides scriptural justification for his Gospel. He artfully weaves into the text of his argument a catena of fourteen references to the Jewish Scriptures: Is 29:16; 45:9; Hos 2:23; 1:10; Is 10:22–23; 1:9; 28:16; Jl 2:32; Is 52:7; 53:1; 19:4; Dt 32:1; Is 65:1; 65:2. The catena begins and ends with texts from Isaiah, and texts from Isaiah form the backbone of the whole into which are interspersed texts from other Scriptures.

We may take Is 65:1, which occurs near the end of this section, to illustrate the way in which the text of Isaiah, read messianically, functions as a scriptural canon for Paul.

When Paul read the words of the Lord in Is 65:1, "I have been found by those who did not seek me; I have shown myself to those who did not ask for me," he did not, as modern scholars do, take these words to refer to apostate Israel, but rather understood them to refer to the Gentiles. Read in this way, Paul could be certain that it was God's will that the Gentiles be saved. Or, at least, it was God's will that they should have the Gospel preached to them. Why else would the Lord show himself to those who did not seek him?

The earthly Jesus may himself never have engaged in a mission to the Gentiles. But, for Paul, the crucified and resurrected Jesus was the Lord, and the Lord could also be heard speaking through the prophet Isaiah. What is found in Isaiah, when read christologically, is normative. We are not to think that the words in Isaiah initiated Paul's work with Gentiles (though this possibility cannot be strictly ruled out). We are rather to imagine, I think, that Paul's experience of the fact that Gentiles were being saved, quite apart from a conscious and deliberate mission to them, opened his eyes to what was there in the Scriptures to be seen by those who had eyes of faith. Clearly it was the Lord's intention that Gentiles be saved!

Paul's call to engage in a mission to the Gentiles became a part of the norm for his Gospel. It was the will of God that this mission proceed in spite of any difficulties it might cause. Beatings, shipwreck, exposure, and imprisonment were all as nothing compared to the privilege of witnessing to the glory of God that had shown forth in the face of Jesus Christ.

Thus arose the conflict over the law, a conflict over what was to norm the corporate life of the Church. As far as Paul was concerned, preaching the glorious Gospel of Jesus Christ was inseparable from preaching to the Gentiles. Yet, the law required that Jews remain separate from Gentiles. Beneath this conflict over the law was a deeper consciousness and experience of the love of God that had been shed abroad by Jesus Christ in the hearts of both Jews and Gentiles.

The fact remains, however, that it was not Jesus but the apostles who worked through the problem of the law so that Gentiles could be admitted into the Church without circumcision. Or perhaps we can say that this was accomplished by Jesus *and* the apostles. Or, to be more precise, it was the achievement of "the word of the Lord" and the apostles. In other words, in this instance, a new problem had arisen for which there was no "word of the Lord" and Christian prophets had to speak for him in the apostolic councils where this question was eventually resolved. This underscores that there have been an untold number of life-giving "words of the Lord" spoken in the Spirit of Jesus that have made decisive contributions to the expediting of the Gospel that have not been handed down in the Church.

The fact, however, that the achievement of the full admission of the Gentiles was worked out with the decisive participation of the apostles meant that *any canon of Scriptures adequate for the needs of*

*the Gentile Church could only be a canon that made clear the role of
the apostles in carrying on and extending to the Gentiles the work begun by Jesus and his disciples.*

(2) *The Apostolic Presence of Paul*

While Paul never envisioned a new canon of Scripture that
would feature a collection of his letters, his Churches knew that his
letters carried his apostolic presence. Paul wrote to the Church in
Corinth that he did not want to appear to be frightening them with
his letters. He explains that his opponents say that "his letters are
weighty and strong, but his bodily presence is weak, and his speech
of no account." He then proceeds to warn the Corinthian Christians:
"Let such people understand that what we say by letter when absent,
we do when present" (2 Cor 10:9).

This means that Paul's letters, at least those that were written
with this purpose in mind (and all that have been preserved appear
to meet this standard), represented his apostolic presence.[59] One reason Paul was able to accomplish so much was that he did not need to
visit personally every Church that needed his guidance. His letters
had the power to represent his presence. For those who would accept
them as such, Paul need only write letters and thus save the time and
energy required to travel and make personal visits.

A collection of Paul's letters would have served to make power-
fully present in the Churches which possessed them the apostolic
presence of the apostle to the Gentiles, if only they could be properly
edited and placed in the hands of people who remembered the apostle and could authoritatively interpret their meaning. It was virtually
assured, once these letters were collected and began circulating as a
corpus, that any new canon of Christian Scripture adequate for the
use of Gentile Churches would include these writings. They made
clear the decisive contribution of the apostles—above all, of the apostle to the Gentiles.

For the Gentile Church, Jesus without the apostles was mean-
ingless. For these Churches, only "Jesus *and* the Apostles," would
be adequate. The earliest apostolic writings that have been preserved
in the Church are letters of Paul. *Paul's letters, along with the "words
of the Lord," constituted the embryonic beginnings of what eventually
emerged as the New Testament canon.*

(3) *The Gospels, Paul's Letters,*
and the Motif of Martyrdom

Paul's way of giving expression to his conviction that it was God's will that the Gentiles be saved was to assert that Christ died for all—Jews and Gentiles alike. Thus, for Paul, the death of Christ, or the cross of Christ, meant an end to the normativity of the law that God had given to Moses on Mount Sinai (at least as far as the Church is concerned). Through Christ comes a new creation—neither Jew nor Gentile, neither slave nor free, neither male nor female. Salvation is open to all who by faith trust in the righteousness of God who justifies the sinner—both Jew and Gentile.

All of the Gospels that have been included in the canon of the Christian Church embrace this Pauline doctrine of salvation for Gentiles apart from the law. The words of Jesus are incorporated into Gospels featuring not only the teachings of Jesus as "words of the Lord," but also his passion and death on a cross, and his resurrection and exaltation as the messianic Son of God.

The Gospels already presage the uniting of the two basic elements of the New Testament, i.e., the "words of the Lord" and the witness of the apostles to the death and resurrection of Jesus for the salvation of all who enter into the new covenant of faith. The Gospels invite and call for discipleship. They are apologetic missionary writings proclaiming the good news of God's salvation for all. Once they are brought into relationship with the letters of Paul, however, they will become something more. They will provide the model for imitation. When Paul writes, "Be ye imitators of me, as I am of Christ," he had in mind the self-emptying love of Christ. But by the time Paul's letters were collected, Paul had imitated his Savior by undergoing martyrdom at the hands of the Roman authorities. Ignatius, who is the first to base his teaching on both the letters of Paul and the Gospels, concluded that imitating Christ meant, above all, imitating the passion and martyrdom of Jesus.

The influence of Ignatius and Polycarp, both profound students of Paul's letters and the Gospels, established a tradition that in imitating Paul as Paul had imitated Christ, one reads both Paul's letters and the Gospels in order to learn how to be "Christian" martyrs. *In a tradition which honors the memory of the martyred apostles, Peter, Paul, and James, to read the Gospels and Paul's letters together is to move decisively, even if inadvertently, in the direction of a martyr's canon.* The purpose of these martyrdoms is to rekindle apostolic faith and keep alive the "apostolic presence."

With Ignatius and Polycarp we have the authentic root of the particular tradition of martyrdom that strongly influenced the formation of the New Testament. Irenaeus not only was a disciple of Polycarp, but also regarded Ignatius as a model for Christian martyrdom. In *Against Heresies* 5.28.4, Irenaeus wrote:

> As a certain man of ours said, when he was condemned to the wild beasts because of his witness to God: "I am the wheat of Christ, and am ground by the teeth of the wild beasts, that I may be found the pure bread of God."

Irenaeus' use of the words of Ignatius found in Ignatius' *Letter to the Romans* (chapter 4) removes all doubt concerning the origins of the tradition of martyrdom received and handed on by Irenaeus. It came from the East, from Asia Minor and Syria. It was embodied in Polycarp of Smyrna and Ignatius of Antioch. As we see clearly in the example of Ignatius, however, this was a tradition that was oriented toward Rome, and the martyrdom there of the apostles Peter and Paul.

2. THE CONCEPTUAL IMPORTANCE OF LUKE-ACTS

a. The Necessity of "Acts of the Apostles"

One thing the Gospels do not and cannot do is to make explicit a particular matter that is implicit in them. The Gospels do not make explicit the decisive circumstance under which Gentiles were admitted into the Church apart from the works of the law. This means that the Gospels themselves, while they represent the apostolic witness to the death and resurrection of Jesus, cannot do justice to the full importance of the apostles. Without the "apostolic presence" the Gentiles would never have heard the Gospel of Christ. The fact that an adequate Christian canon must make clear the decisive contribution of the apostles was well understood by the author of Luke-Acts.

John Knox has argued convincingly that the author of Luke-Acts must have known of the letters of Paul. According to Knox, the fact that the author of Acts makes no mention of Paul as a letter writer, and, so far as we can tell, shows no evidence of dependence on these letters, indicates that he has chosen to ignore them. This is best explained if we imagine the author of Luke-Acts living at a time and in a Church where Paul's letters are being used in a way that renders them of dubious value for his purposes.[60]

The author of Luke-Acts was not prepared to allow his Church to be dependent on Paul's letters for its understanding of the apostolic contribution to salvation history. Any tendency to exalt the contribution of a particular apostle above all others was to be corrected by the work of this author. Above all, any tendency to exaggerate the conflict between Peter and Paul or between Paul and the apostles in Jerusalem was to be corrected. The unity of the Church was to be underlined. The author of Luke-Acts brought together the two chief apostles, Peter and Paul. Acts especially shows how the Gospel was carried first to the Jews and then to the Gentiles. It also clarifies for the Gentile reader how the Gospel of Jesus Christ which began with Jesus and his disciples in Judea and Galilee was connected with the Gospel that had been preached to them by the apostles.

b. The Pre-Marcionite Roman Canon

Luke-Acts was especially useful to the Christian Church in Rome, for it showed how the apostle Paul reached Rome. It also explained Paul's relationship to those who were apostles before him. From these earlier apostles had come those who first preached the Gospel in Rome. Any Church that knew Paul mainly through his Epistle to the Romans and remembered his martyrdom in Rome would have appreciated Luke-Acts. The emphasis upon the importance of concord within the Church at the end of Paul's Epistle to the Romans accords well with the overall position of the author of Luke-Acts.

The Acts of the Apostles was never, so far as we know, of any scriptural importance outside of Rome until after the middle of the second century. Its first explicit use is in the letter from the Rhone Valley to the Churches of Asia concerning the martyrs of Gaul. Ori-

gen, possibly under the influence of Rome or the writings of Irenaeus, acknowledged it as a part of the New Testament canon in the
third century. If the Gospels were written after A.D. 70, and if the
external evidence for a Roman provenance for the Gospel of Mark is
reliable, then the use of the speeches of Peter in Acts by the author of
Mark affords the best explanation both for the tradition closely asso-
ciating the apostle Peter with the Gospel of Mark and for the shape
and content of Mark.

Assuming the reliability of the scholarly consensus dating Matthew and Luke after A.D. 70, and the likelihood of the common authorship of Luke-Acts, and assuming the reliability of the external
evidence supporting a Roman provenance for Mark, if, as appears
probable, Mark was written after Matthew and Luke-Acts, then
Mark's use of Acts would be the earliest external evidence for the
date and provenance of Luke-Acts. We conclude that Luke-Acts was
known in Rome at the time the Gospel of Mark was written.[61]

After the Gospel of Mark was written there was in Rome a
"proto-canon" of Christian Scriptures including at least the Gospels
of Matthew and Mark, the two-volume work Luke-Acts, and Paul's
Epistle to the Romans. What other Christian writings may have been
circulating in Rome at this time is difficult to conjecture. But even
these books alone make up a full one-half of the eventual New Testament canon that finally developed. These books constitute a very important core of writings that could easily have developed into the list
of books included in Irenaeus' New Testament. All that is needed is
the addition of more letters of Paul, letters of other apostles, the
Gospel of John, and the Revelation of John.

3. MARCION

Marcion was born about A.D. 85. So, when he came to Rome c.
140, he was in his fifties and probably had long since worked out the
basic essentials of his program. It is presumed that he brought with
him to Rome his copy of a collection of Paul's letters. He may also
have brought with him the Gospel he edited from the Gospel of
Luke. The need for his Gospel must have been apparent to him for a
long time before he reached Rome.

a. Marcion's Gospel

From what we can learn indirectly about Marcion from references to his work by others, it appears that his Gospel was as freely edited as had been the Gospels of Matthew, Luke, and Mark. There is no evidence that his Gospel included tradition that was not present in either Matthew or Luke. In this regard Marcion's Gospel was similar to Mark. Like Mark, his Gospel had no birth narratives and omitted precious "words of the Lord" like the Lord's Prayer and the parable of the lost son. Most of the tradition in Marcion's Gospel is found in the Gospel of Luke. Tertullian is convinced that Marcion created his Gospel out of Luke by making major and unwarranted excisions from Luke. Marcion's Gospel is clearly shorter than Luke, and also shorter than Matthew. We cannot say, however, that Marcion's Gospel is a simple editing of Luke. It appears to have contained some tradition that is found only in Matthew.

John Knox notes that "Marcion's text is undoubtedly nearer Matthew and Mark than is Luke."[62] Harnack suggested that there was in Rome a text of Luke which had been corrected to the text of Matthew and Mark.[63]

All that we can be certain of is that Marcion's Gospel was the fourth Synoptic Gospel. Marcion recognized the distinction between Matthew, Mark and Luke, on the one hand, and John on the other. His decision to compose his Gospel as he did was a decision against the Gospel of John. This was an act of courage for the son of a Christian bishop in Asia Minor. The Gospel of John was the Gospel of Asia Minor. This is clear from the debate that arose over the date of Easter. The churches of Asia Minor, following the Gospel of John, celebrated Easter on the assumption that the death of Jesus occurred on the preparation day for the feast of Passover, i.e., the fourteenth day of the Jewish month Nisan. The other Churches in the Roman empire followed the tradition of celebrating Easter always on the first day of the week, without worrying about conforming this date too exactly to the Jewish calendar. The attempt was made to observe Easter on the first Sunday following the Jewish Passover since the death of Jesus did indeed occur during the period that Jews were in Jerusalem for the Passover festival. This practice seemed to meet fully the requirements set by the texts of Matthew, Mark and Luke.

The difference that developed between the observance of Easter in Asia Minor and that which developed outside of Asia Minor caused great difficulties in the days of Victor, bishop of Rome, who, on the grounds of this difference, temporarily excommunicated the Churches of Asia Minor.[64]

We may presume that Marcion's Gospel, turning its back on the Gospel of John in its overall approach to the Gospel tradition, would have made Marcion appear disloyal and rash in Asia Minor. According to legend the leading bishop of Asia Minor, Polycarp of Smyrna, once referred to him as a "son of Satan."

Marcion was a shipowner and merchant. In this capacity he had occasion to travel about the Mediterranean and learn about Christian Churches outside his native region. As the ancient Greek geographers and historians had earlier sailed the eastern Mediterranean inquiring about the sources of the great rivers and the origin of religious customs in different countries, so it would appear that Marcion, the second Christian *histor* (the first being, I am assuming, the author of Luke-Acts), made inquiries about Christian origins and sources that led him to remap the world of Christian theology in ways that eventually made him unpopular at home.

There need be no mystery as to why Marcion seems to have chosen Luke as his basic source for his reconstructed Gospel. If he was set on finding the truth about Christian beginnings, he was standing in the tradition of the author of Luke-Acts. It would have been in accord with his purposes to begin with that Gospel whose author had avowedly the same end in view. Also, Marcion's preoccupation with the primitive Pauline corpus is explained well in terms of an aim to study the second volume of Luke-Acts in the light of earlier and more original sources.

Since Marcion's father was a bishop of the Church (and we know of no question about his father's orthodoxy), it may be presumed that Marcion grew up with a Johannine tradition. Though there is little if any evidence on the point, it is not unnatural to conclude that Marcion's first departures from that tradition were consequent to theological reflection stimulated by the wider perspective that came with travel and the affluence to support his private research.

We are not to think that when he arrived in Rome it was his

first visit to that great Mediterranean city and important Christian Church. We are, rather, to view that arrival in c. A.D. 140 as Marcion's conscious move as a Christian reformer to actualize change in the Church of his fathers.

The date of around A.D. 85 for the birth of Marcion appears to be quite defensible.[65] Thus, he would have been a grown man by A.D. 105, and well along in life when the renewed outbreak of war between the Jews and Romans took place in Judaea in A.D. 135. Many Jews were convinced that Bar Cochba was the long-awaited Messiah. This raised questions for thinking Christians that had never been raised before—at least not with the sense of historical urgency posed by the Bar Cochba revolt. It is likely that it was at this time that Marcion became acutely aware of the fact that the Scriptures of the Jews could be read as a history of the Jewish nation, and that the traditional way of reading these Scriptures in the Church was certainly not the only way to read them, and perhaps not the best way.

Marcion was in the prime of life four years later when he consciously moved his base of operations to Rome. Jerusalem, where Paul had laid his Gospel before those who were apostles before him, was in ruins. Where is the leadership of the Church to which a Paul *redivivus* can appeal if not Rome? Rome was not only at the crossroads of the empire, but the city where the blessed Paul had been taken after his rejection by the authorities in Jerusalem. In going to Rome, Marcion was following Paul.

At first, Marcion was accepted in Rome. No doubt, Rome offered fertile ground for pressing his case against the Mosaic law and against what he regarded as Judaizing interpolations introduced into Paul's letters and the Gospel of Luke. Rome also would have been hospitable to his enthusiasm for the apostle Paul and to his championing of the Pauline corpus which, until that time, may not have been regarded in Rome as a discrete collection of Scriptures. Marcion developed a strong case against regarding the God of the Jews as the God of the Christians. Rome was a city in which this case, at least at first, could have been listened to with real interest.

Marcion responded to his acceptance by the Church in Rome with a large gift. (Compare Paul's agreement to raise money for the saints in Jerusalem after the acceptance of his Gospel by the pillars of the church in Jerusalem.) This gift was in the form of a donation of 200,000 sesterces (well over one million dollars). This sum may be exaggerated, for it is a very large amount of money. We may be confident, however, that Marcion's gift was substantial. So far as is known, it was the largest single contribution ever made to a Christian Church up until that time. There is every reason to believe that Marcion, like Paul before him, was making a conscious bid for power in the apostolic Church. It is difficult to imagine that this bold move to Rome had nothing to do with the bloody upheaval caused in the eastern Mediterranean world by the messianic uprising of the Jews, only recently suppressed by the Romans.[66] The emperor had unequivocally banished all Jews from Judea. This had resulted in an enormous displacement of the Jewish population (including Jewish Christians in Jerusalem) which must have created refugee problems throughout the Mediterranean world. Tensions between Jews and the native population of all Mediterranean cities naturally heightened dramatically.

Not since the bloody conflict of A.D. 66–70, which had resulted in the destruction of the temple in Jerusalem and the dismantling of the Jewish state, had the Pauline Gospel (over against the more Jewish interpretations of Christian faith) been so evidently vindicated by the apparent course of historical events. As the fall of Jerusalem in A.D. 70 had resulted in a great resurgence of Paulinism among postwar Christian churches,[67] so also, we may be confident, there was a renewal of confidence in the rightness of Paul's vision following the events of A.D. 135. We must imagine what it meant for an affluent well-traveled, devoted Paulinist, just turning fifty, to listen to reports about the final crushing blow of the Roman state against the flesh of Abraham, and to hear about the decision to build a Hellenistic temple on Mount Zion. We know that Marcion was absorbed in the question of the relationship between Christianity and Judaism. These events must have riveted his attention and forced him to reflect on their significance. The irrepressible Jewish hope in a Messiah, and the belief of many that Bar Cochba *was* the expected Messiah of the Jewish Scriptures, would have led anyone interested in Christian origins to the deepest kind of reflection and to ponder the most radical of Christian options. The Jewish Scriptures bore witness to the history of the Jewish nation. That nation, all reasonable men would have been prone to conclude, was now *finis*.

Marcion went to Rome convinced that the God and Father of Jesus Christ had nothing to do with the God worshiped by the Jews. As a merchant and shipbuilder, Marcion understood very well the benefits of the *Pax Romana.* The fortune he turned over to the Church at Rome was far more than most men were able to earn in a lifetime, let alone save. His business had flourished. He had felt the issues that had been raised by the religious war in Judea, not only in his mind and heart, but in his pocketbook. From his head to the soles of his feet, Marcion had been radicalized in mid-life, and he had made his decision, which was to engage in an all-out effort to persuade the Church to disown its Jewish heritage.

Marcion's bitterest opponent, Tertullian, a generation later, was to ask, "What has Jerusalem to do with Athens?" The question Marcion posed for Christians was, "What has the Gospel to do with Jerusalem?" No doubt, in the aftermath of the Bar Cochba uprising, this was for a time regarded as a discussible question. But, in due course, it became apparent in the Church that the implications of this question, as posed by Marcion, were far too radical. In about A.D. 144, after a hearing before the presbytery of the Church in Rome, which met at his request, Marcion was expelled. Marcion went on to spend a prolonged period of more than fourteen years carrying on missionary activity in the Mediterranean world, not neglecting Rome which continued to be a fertile mission field for him even after his excommunication.[68]

b. Marcion's Canon

Marcion created for the use of his Churches a Christian canon that was made up of Christian writings only. Over against the "Old Testament," Marcion produced a document called "The Antitheses." This work brought out the conflicts and contradictions between Christian faith and the "Old Testament." We can now appropriately use the term "Old Testament" for the term "the Jewish Scriptures" to refer to the Christian Scriptures the Gentile churches received from the apostles that had been handed down in the earliest communities from Jesus and his disciples. Now, for the first time, these Scriptures are perceived as belonging to the past as far as the Church is concerned. No longer will Christians, influenced by the kind of radical rethinking of the question of canon posed by Marcion, read these writings as they had been read by the apostles, including the apostle Paul. These writings will henceforth, in the eyes of those who no longer regard them as "Christian" Scripture, refer to the covenant which God made with Israel, a covenant now superseded at best, and, in the eyes of Marcionites, invalid for Christians.

It seems likely that Luke-Acts functioned as a model for Marcion's Gospel-apostle. In place of Luke, Marcion substituted his "improved" version of that same Gospel. In place of the Acts of the Apostles, Marcion substituted his edited version of a collection of Paul's letters.[69] It is *very significant* that Ephesians apparently headed the list of Paul's letters. The collection had been made and edited by some Paulinist who was confident about the value of stressing a need for the unity that Christians have in Christ, which was to be made manifest in the unity of the Church. Marcion saw a different need, the need for a stress on the freedom that Christians have in Paul's Gospel.

There need be little doubt of Marcion's personal and existential identification with the frustrated, defiant, and undaunted Paul of Galatians. There is no reason to think that Marcion, any more than Paul, was unnecessarily provocative or polemical. He had built up his shipping business because he knew how to plan for the future, organize, and inspire others to work with him toward a common goal. This is one reason he was so successful in founding Churches all over the eastern Mediterranean world. Marcion knew how to get along with others. At times, no doubt, the exhortation for concord that Paul makes at the end of his Letter to the Romans was an ideal that Marcion lifted up for his adherents to follow. But, in laying down the constitution of his Church, which was to begin a movement of reform among Christians, he made the decisive decision to give a prominent place to Paul's Letter to the Galatians.

Like Paul and Luther, Marcion was a man of courage and passion who had worked out his position carefully and had done the work of scholarship to back it up. This position called for radical change, which, understandably, was resisted. When Marcion stood his ground, conflict ensued, and he was expelled from the Church. Where Paul had succeeded, Marcion failed. He did not, in the showdown, carry the leadership of the Church with him.[70]

Marcion, nonetheless, has left his mark on the Church. For the

New Testament canon of the great Church that expelled Marcion is clearly, in part, an expansion and development of the pre-Marcionite Roman canon, made in response to Marcion's new "Gospel-apostle."

4. JUSTIN MARTYR AND TATIAN

Edgar J. Goodspeed opened his chapter on the "Age of Justin" with the following overall picture of the situation in Rome in the period just following Marcion's excommunication, and at the beginning of the great missionary effort to which Marcion devoted the remainder of his life.

> In the middle of the second century, the Christians in Rome (Goodspeed is referring to those who excommunicated Marcion) would gather on Sunday and listen to the reading of the memoirs of the apostles or the writings of the prophets. This is the statement of Justin, who was a member of the Roman Church at that time (*1st Apology* 67.3). Justin was born in Palestine. . . . He became a Christian (in Asia Minor). About 140, he became a Christian teacher, and a few years later went to Rome, where Marcion was already established. By the time Justin reached Rome, Marcion . . . had left the Church and begun the organization of Churches of peculiar Pauline type. With men at Rome like Valentinus, Cerdo, Marcion, Justin, and Tatian, the years that followed were of great significance there.[71]

Goodspeed is convinced that Justin wrote his famous dialogue with Trypho as "a great counterblast to Marcion's *Antitheses*," and he goes on to say, "Marcion maintained that Christianity contradicted the Jewish Scriptures; Justin maintained that it fulfilled them."[72] It does appear that Justin's work could have been conceived as a response to Marcion's program to rid the Church of doctrinal dependence of the Old Testament.

Justin does not specify the names of the apostles whose "Memoirs" were being read in church, but he knows that these documents were composed by "the apostles and by those who followed them." This distinction suggests that he knew that Mark and Luke were not written by apostles but by disciples of apostles. At one point, however, he refers to a statement that is found only in the Gospel of Mark (3:16–17) and says with reference to Peter that it is recorded "in his memoirs" (*Dialogue* 106.3), indicating that he was accustomed to recognize the Gospel of Mark as one of the "memoirs of the apostles" read in church. There is little reason to doubt that the other Gospels he recognized as "memoirs of the apostles" were Matthew, Luke and John. Justin knows other Gospels but he seldom uses them.

The important point is this: at the same time that Roman Christians in Marcionite Churches were learning to read a single, newly reconstructed Gospel, based conservatively on what Marcion believed to be the most original form of the Gospel that Paul read, the Roman Church that had expelled Marcion read no single Gospel. Justin uses the plural: Gospels were being read. This Church was well aware of the differences between the Gospels and of the need for some solution to the problem created for the Church by these differences. So long as only Matthew and Luke were involved, Mark could point the way forward for the Church at Rome, but in Asia Minor the Churches were following the Gospel of John, and this was causing difficulties, as the matter of observing Easter made clear. Justin, though a native of Palestine, had become a Christian in Asia Minor, and for him the Gospel of John was an important apostolic memoir.

The advantage the Marcionite Churches had with a single Gospel that was free of inconsistencies and "Judaistic" interpolations was very real. The whole problem was, no doubt, discussed in Justin's school in Rome. One of his students, Tatian, later, in Syria, after Justin's martyrdom c. 165, published a single unified Gospel which drew together on an inclusive basis almost all of the traditions contained in the Gospels of Matthew, Mark, Luke, and John. It was called *The Diatessaron* because it was one Gospel through four. There is evidence that in Justin's school the words of Jesus were sometimes cited from texts in which sayings found in the Gospels of Matthew and Luke had been conflated or harmonized.[73]

Justin was the first writer to mention the Revelation of John. He believed it to have been written by the apostle John (*Dialogue* 81.4).

It was in Rome from about the middle of the second century that Christian Churches had the experience of what might be termed "well-organized denominational competition." It was in this competitive situation that the pre-Marcionite Roman canon developed into the first post-Marcionite "Catholic" canon. If the Gospel of John was not already used in Rome in the earlier period, it now begins to be recognized as an apostolic Gospel. If the Revelation of John was not used in Rome in the earlier period, it now begins to gain recognition as a book written by the apostle John.

By the time of Justin, the Christian Scriptures known and used in Rome included about two-thirds of the eventual content of the New Testament. What mainly remained to be done was (1) to separate Luke and Acts, (2) to place Luke with Matthew, Mark, and John in a fourfold Gospel canon, (3) to embrace Marcion's ten letter Pauline corpus, expanding it with other letters of the apostle Paul and letters of other apostles, and (4) to retain Acts as a bridge between the fourfold Gospel canon and the expanded corpus of apostolic letters.

What was to be the next development? How was it to take place?

5. POLYCARP, MARTYR AND BISHOP OF SMYRNA

In the Book of Revelation, the Christian prophet John, in response to heavenly instruction, wrote to the Church in Smyrna as follows:

> I know your tribulation and your poverty (but you are rich) and the slander of those who say that they are Jews and are not, but are a synagogue of Satan. Do not fear what you are about to suffer. Behold, the devil is about to throw some of you into prison, that you may be tested, and for ten days you will have tribulation. Be faithful unto death, and I will give you the crown of life. He who has an ear to hear, let him hear what the Spirit says to the Churches. He who conquers shall not be hurt by the second death (2:9–11).

"Be faithful unto death, and I will give you the crown of life." What fateful words for a city to hear!

When Ignatius, bishop of Antioch, was on his way to a martyr's death in Rome, he was able to persuade those who held him in protective custody to stop in Smyrna. There he visited with Polycarp, bishop of Smyrna. Later, from Troas, Ignatius wrote a letter to the Church in Smyrna in which he greeted the Smyrneans in the following words:

> ... I have perceived that you are established in faith immovable, being as it were nailed on the cross of the Lord, Jesus Christ, in flesh and in spirit, and firmly grounded in love in the blood of Christ, fully persuaded as touching our Lord that he is truly of the race of David, according to the flesh ... truly nailed up in the flesh for our sakes under Pontius Pilate and Herod the tetrarch. . . .
>
> He suffered all these things for our sakes; and he suffered truly ... not as certain unbelievers say, that he suffered in semblance. . . .
>
> If these things were done by our Lord in semblance, then am I also a prisoner in semblance. And why then have I delivered myself over to death, unto fire, unto sword, unto wild beasts? But near to the sword, near to God, in company with wild beasts, in company with God. Only let it be in the name of Jesus Christ, so that we may suffer together with him. I endure all things, seeing that he himself, who is perfect man, enableth me (1–4).

At the same time, Ignatius sent a letter to his younger episcopal colleague, Polycarp, in which he wrote:

> Be sober, as God's athlete. The prize is incorruption and life eternal, concerning which thou also art persuaded. In all things I am devoted to thee—I and my bonds which thou didst cherish.
>
> Let not those that seem to be plausible and yet teach strange doctrine dismay thee. Stand thou firm, as an anvil when it is smitten. It is the part of a great athlete to receive blows and be victorious. But especially must we, for God's sake, endure all things, that he may endure us. Await him

... who suffered for our sake, who endured in all ways for our sake (2–3).

It was many years later at the advanced age of eighty-six, that the bishop of Smyrna was martyred along with other Christians in Smyrna. The Church in Smyrna, sensing the great importance of the death of its bishop, drew up a letter that was intended for wide circulation. It reads, in part, as follows:

> We write unto you, brethren, an account of what befell those that suffered martyrdom, and especially the blessed Polycarp, who put an end to the persecution by sealing it, so to speak, with his own martyrdom. For, nearly all the foregoing events came to pass that the Lord might show us once more an example of martyrdom which is conformable to the Gospel. For he waited to be betrayed, just as the Lord did, to the end that we also might be imitators of him. . . .
>
> These things then happened with so great speed, quicker than words can tell, the crowds forthwith collecting from the workshops and baths timber and faggots, and the Jews being especially zealous, as usual, to assist with this. . . .
>
> So it befell the blessed Polycarp. . . . He showed himself not only a notable teacher, but also a distinguished martyr, whose martyrdom all desire to imitate, seeing that it was after the pattern of the Gospel of Christ. Having by his endurance overcome the unrighteous ruler in the conflict and so received the crown of immortality. . . .

A colophon attached to the end of the extant copies of this letter indicates that we have in our possession copies that go back to a copy of this letter that reached the hands of Irenaeus, who, according to tradition, was in Rome when Polycarp was martyred. This letter was read in the churches of Gaul on a regular basis.

Before his death, Polycarp made an important trip to Rome. Irenaeus, as a young man, had been a disciple of Polycarp. Whether

Irenaeus was with Polycarp during the visit to Rome is not known. But Irenaeus certainly visited Rome from Gaul, and there can be little doubt that between these two native sons of Asia Minor there was also an important Roman connection. Nor can there be any doubt that this Roman connection was important for the development of the New Testament canon.[74]

Fortunately we have reliable knowledge of Polycarp's choice of Christian Scriptures. Not long after Ignatius had written him from Troas, Polycarp received a letter from the Church in Philippi. Ignatius had asked the Philippians to write a letter of encouragement to the Church in Antioch. The Philippians indicated in their letter to Polycarp that they had written such a letter and that they were sending it by way of Smyrna with the hope that Polycarp would arrange to have it forwarded to its destination. They also asked Polycarp whether he would send them copies of any letters of Ignatius that he might have. In his reply to the Philippians, Polycarp disclaims any expert knowledge of the Scripture. But this disclaimer clearly refers to the Jewish Scriptures handed down from Jesus and his disciples. His own letter is full of phrases and expressions from New Testament books. According to Bishop J.B. Lightfoot's edition of the *Apostolic Fathers*,[75] there are a total of forty-six New Testament allusions in the text of Polycarp's letter: five from Matthew, two from Mark, one from Luke, two from Acts, two from Romans, four from 1 Corinthians, three from 2 Corinthians, four from Galatians, four from Ephesians, two from Philippians, two from 2 Thessalonians, three from 1 Timothy, two from 2 Timothy, nine from 1 Peter, and one from 1 John.

What is striking on first glance is the absence of any reference to two of the most important books from the Churches of Asia, the Gospel of John and the Revelation of John. It has been suggested that Polycarp disliked the chiliasm of the Revelation of John. But at the same time, he could hardly allow that to override the fact that this book marked out the Church of Smyrna as one of the seven churches of Asia to be addressed by Christ himself. And Polycarp's stand on the date of Easter makes it clear that the Gospel of John had great authority for him. It is to be concluded, therefore, that Polycarp may have made no reference to these books deliberately. Perhaps it was the diplomatic thing to do. Both books were in different ways troublesome and caused no little conflict in various parts of the Church.

The frequent references to Paul's letters are notable. This includes Ephesians and 1 and 2 Timothy. 1 Peter gets special attention, and the single reference to 1 John is important. Two possible allusions to Acts are also of importance. It is striking that there appear to be no allusions to any Christian writings that later were rejected as heretical. There can be little doubt that Polycarp's library of Christian writings is the purest touchstone that we have of the emerging New Testament canon that is later evidenced in the writings of Irenaeus, the critical reflections of Origen, and the literary and historical investigations of Eusebius.

It was in the very period when Justin published his counterblast against Marcion that Polycarp made what so far as we know was his one and only trip to Rome. The purpose of his trip was to visit Anicetus, the bishop of Rome. The trip was made c. A.D. 154–155.

Ernst Barnikol traced the "birth" of the Catholic Church to this episcopal conference.[76] He claimed that previous to this unprecedented meeting of bishops from East and West, orthodox Christianity had possessed no monarchical episcopate, no New Testament canon, and no creed; it had made no parallelism between the apostles Peter and Paul; in fact, it had ignored Paul. Barnikol concluded that the importance of the meeting lay in the probability that the two bishops agreed to make common cause against the threat of Marcion. The expression "orthodox Christianity" is troublesome in this context, and one might want to take exception to some of what Barnikol claimed. For example, the Acts of the Apostles makes a parallelism of sorts between the apostles Peter and Paul. And what was Ignatius if not a monarchical bishop? However, Barnikol's suggestion that the two bishops agreed to make common cause against Marcion appears altogether probable.

6. THE FOURFOLD GOSPEL CANON

From a letter written by Irenaeus a generation after Polycarp met Anicetus in Rome, we learn that, in spite of the disagreement between the two bishops over the date of Easter, a disagreement they never resolved, the two men remained united in the faith and shared the Eucharist. The practical consequence of this agreement to disagree over this portentous ecclesiastical problem which divided the Church was to bind the Gospel of John (from Asia Minor) to the Gospels of Matthew, Mark, and Luke (from the Church at large) into an ecumenical Gospel canon.[77] Justin and Valentinus, representing quite different traditions, had already brought attention in Rome to the theological importance of the Gospel of John.

It is not important whether it was exactly at this time that the four Gospels were copied into a single codex where each Gospel was introduced with the same titular formula: "The Gospel According to . . ." What is important is this: so far as is known, there was no other moment in Church history when it is more likely that the fourfold Gospel canon was, in principle, implicitly agreed upon. The Gospel of John, so different from the Gospel of Matthew, figuratively speaking, is to be henceforth bound together with the Gospel according to Matthew, along with that according to Mark and that according to Luke, into one common inspired corpus, which, with all its diversity, is to be perceived as a fourfold witness to the one and only apostolic and Catholic Gospel. The decision reached in principle is this: neither the separate Gospels of Matthew, Mark, Luke, or John, nor any combinations of any two or three of these Gospels will provide the ultimate Gospel norm for Christian faith and practice. Rather, the Catholic and ecumenical Church now has one apostolic Gospel for which it has four witnesses—that according to Matthew, that according to Mark, that according to Luke, and that according to John.

In order to create the new theological construct that was to symbolize and represent the newly actualized reality of diversity in unity that henceforth was to unite the Churches of Asia Minor and the Churches in communion with Rome, it was necessary *for the first time* (so far as is known) for the Catholic Church to separate the Gospel of Luke from the Acts of the Apostles. Here was an overriding, compelling, theological reason for what otherwise would have been an unwarranted dismantling, if not a disruptive tearing apart of a very important theological construct which had served the Church well: Luke-Acts, i.e., "Gospel and apostle."

Visually perceived in terms of our printed Bibles, it would appear that Luke and Acts could have been kept together by the simple device of placing the Gospel of Luke fourth in the series of Gospels, followed by Acts. But, in the second century, the publication of the fourfold Gospel corpus, conceptually at least, necessitated the separation of Luke and Acts.

It is not unreasonable to think that this conscious act of separation was agreed to in part with the understanding that it would henceforth free the Acts of the Apostles for a greater service. No longer would Acts be perceived as simply the second volume of a two-volume "Gospel-apostle." Now it was free for a new service. It was free to serve to unite conceptually not only the Gospel of Luke with the work of the apostles, but an enlarged ecumenical corpus of four Gospels, including Luke, with a newly created collection of apostolic writings, including, but going far beyond, the Pauline corpus. Here was a canon that could compete successfully with that of Marcion. Marcion's reconstructed Gospel of Luke was dwarfed in the eyes of the Church by the new fourfold Gospel canon, physically, spiritually, and conceptually.

The creation of the fourfold Gospel canon and the separation of Luke-Acts were not two separate acts. The one entailed the other. The trade-off was mutually beneficial to all parties concerned. It was a literary theological illustration of the truism "to die is to live." Both Luke and Acts and the Church for which they were originally composed together have benefited from the sacrifice of their separation. It is notable that in the process no attempt was made to remove the editorial evidence in each that these two books were once one. The Church that formed this new "Catholic" canon would eschew further editorial alteration of the books that had been handed down. This appears to have been, in the long run, a very important decision in light of what Marcion was openly doing.

Marcion made the results of his own critical reflection normative for his Churches by the way he edited his New Testament canon. The framers of the new "Catholic" canon were no less involved in critical reflection. But their actions preserved a much greater scope of freedom for the theologians of the Church, and a much greater responsibility for them as well. Irenaeus is the first known Catholic theologian to step in and creatively exercise this freedom and new-found responsibility.

7. BASILIDES AND VALENTINUS

Before Irenaeus could make his contribution it was necessary for the Church to experience even further challenges than those posed by Marcion or by official persecution. These challenges came from Egypt in the form of Christian-Gnostic theological reflection, writing, teaching and influence.

Basilides taught in Alexandria during the period when the Jews under Bar Cochba were raising the banner of Jewish freedom and sovereignty in neighboring Judea. It must have been an especially difficult time for Christians in Egypt, since it is intrinsically probable that the populace there was once more being called upon to make wartime sacrifices in putting down a dangerous Jewish threat to the stability and security of the eastern frontier of the Roman empire. Some of the same pressures that worked upon Marcion were also at work upon Basilides and Valentinus. However, in Alexandria there was the Philonic tradition of allegorizing Moses and the prophets. This prepared the way for a similar approach to the Gospels and Paul's letters. In Syria and Asia Minor in the figures of Ignatius and Polycarp, we are treated to more than mere glimpses of a Christian tradition of engaging the world, just as Jesus had engaged the authorities in Jerusalem and Paul eventually engaged them in Rome. From Egypt we are exposed to a different early second-century Christian tradition, one of non-engagement of the world.

Valentinus traveled to Rome, but, unlike Ignatius, Polycarp, Justin Martyr and even Marcion, who all had in mind the dominical and apostolic example of action for God in the world, Valentinus appears to have been in Rome primarily to obtain a wider hearing for his ideas.

Until the recent discovery of the Nag Hammadi materials in Egypt, we have been almost solely dependent upon hostile witnesses to the teaching of the Christian Gnostics. The work of reconstructing the history and significance of Christian Gnosticism on the basis of these documents is still under way.[78] Meanwhile, it is possible to confirm that Basilides and the disciples of Valentinus accepted and used: (1) the Scriptures handed on to the Church by Jesus and his disciples, (2) the Gospels of Matthew, Mark, Luke, and John, plus some others, and (3) the letters of Paul. Moreover, these Christian scholars produced a corpus of exegetical literature based upon these writings. It was this literature that gave scope for the philosophical and theological development of their Gnostic systems.[79]

There is no evidence, however, to indicate that these Christians from Egypt had very much direct influence upon the formation of the "Catholic" New Testament. They clearly accepted and used many of the same basic books that circulated as Scriptures and Christian writings in the rest of the Christian community. They contributed many of their own books, which were in turn used by Christians of their own persuasion. But their main contribution to the formation of the "Catholic" New Testament was by way of providing a challenge to the realistic, action-oriented, world-engaging interpretation of Christian faith championed by Ignatius, Polycarp, Justin Martyr, the martyrs of Gaul, and Irenaeus.

In taking up and overcoming this challenge, it was necessary for "Catholic" theologians like Irenaeus to discredit the special books used by these Christian Gnostic thinkers and writers. This resulted in a refining process of selection that did eventually have an effect upon the shape of the "Catholic" New Testament.

Valentinus had come to Rome in the midst of the conflict over Marcion. At one point he may have had hope of becoming the bishop of Rome.[80] His scriptural interests in Paul and John, no doubt, played some part in the deliberations that went on. The fourfold Gospel canon would have been inclusive of his theological interests in John, while at the same time reminding the Church of the importance of the other three—and relegating to a lesser status the plethora of other Gospels that had been written and were circulating in the churches, like the *Gospel of Thomas,* the *Gospel of Peter,* etc.

The new "Catholic" canon that was emerging in the Church should be viewed as being both a uniting canon (bringing together East and West) and an excluding canon (shutting out certain individuals and groups with their special books).

8. IRENAEUS

Irenaeus was an immigrant from Asia Minor and had known Polycarp as a young man. It is possible that, before settling in Lyons, Irenaeus "had spent time in Rome and had known Justin."[81] When later, as bishop of Lyons, Irenaeus wrote to Victor, bishop of Rome, remonstrating with him concerning the excommunication of the Churches of Asia Minor over the question of dating Easter, he reminded Victor of how differently his predecessor Anicetus had behaved when Polycarp was in Rome. If Irenaeus did spend time in Rome and was there when Justin was there, it is quite possible that he was present when his teacher Polycarp arrived, and that he had first-hand accounts of the understandings reached between the parties of Polycarp and Anicetus. This would help explain why later in his writings as bishop, he championed the apostolic traditions of both Asia Minor and Rome, and why, when it was threatened, he would attempt to preserve the unity that had been forged between these two traditions in connection with Polycarp's visit to Rome. But it does not really matter whether Irenaeus was personally in Rome during this crucial period or not. Since he was the bishop of the martyrs of Lyons, he could not have been unmindful of the instances of martyrdom that followed Polycarp's visit to Rome, both in Rome and in Smyrna. Justin was martyred in Rome in 165. Polycarp seems to have been martyred in Smyrna at about the same time.[82]

By far the simplest solution that can be offered to explain the New Testament canon of the martyrs of Gaul, which was so close to that of Irenaeus, is to see it as a united East-West response to Marcion and the Docetic tendencies present in Gnosticism. This canon had been negotiated in principle in conversations involving representatives from both East and West in the period between A.D. 150 and A.D. 170. We only know about the meetings of the two representative bishops, Polycarp and Anicetus, inadvertently. Had Irenaeus not written his remonstrating letter many years after the event, and had Eusebius failed to include what Irenaeus had written in his *Ecclesiastical History*, we would not even know about this one conference. There probably were numerous discussions before certain fundamental solutions were agreed upon.

There probably was no one dramatic meeting when everything was decided, but there must have been breakthroughs that came with creative ideas, like the fourfold Gospel canon. Could that idea have come from a young expert in the party of the bishop of Smyrna?

In any case, the work was done by leaders who were inclusive in their approach, but capable of drawing lines when they were convinced that essentials of the faith were at stake.

9. THE COLLECTION OF PAUL'S LETTERS

a. Onesimus, Bishop of Ephesus

The collection of Paul's letters is the one major contribution to the New Testament canon yet to be discussed. This contribution was made in the East, in Asia Minor. It is impossible to appreciate fully the dynamic of what happened in Rome after the arrival of Marcion without considering this topic.[83]

When Ignatius was on his way to Rome, and was still some distance from Smyrna, knowing that he would not pass through Ephesus, he sent messengers ahead, along an alternate route, to inform Christians there that he would stop in Smyrna on his way to Troas. The bishop of Ephesus, in spite of his advanced age, decided to make the two-day trip to Smyrna to meet Ignatius and to assure him of his prayers and brotherly concern. Ignatius was moved greatly by this particular visitor, as well he should have been. For, if John Knox is right, and I am persuaded that he is right, this elderly man was none other than the slave concerning whom the apostle Paul wrote his Epistle to Philemon. Moreover, this person appears to have been the one who collected and published Paul's letters.

The destruction of Jerusalem in A.D. 70 would have provided reason enough for some Paulinist to collect and publish Paul's letters, since they exhibit a form of the faith that is not tied to the temple in Jerusalem or to the temporal fate of the Jewish nation. For that matter, the martyrdom of Paul in the previous decade could have effected a similar practical result. However, on the basis of traces of widespread use of Paul's letters, including Ephesians, it is conjectured that the collection of Paul's letters, whenever actually first made, began to receive wide circulation during the closing decade of the first century. More than that we cannot say about the date of the collection.

But what are the reasons for thinking that it was Onesimus, bishop of Ephesus, who made the collection?

(1) Ignatius, in his letter to the Ephesians, written after this vis-

it, clearly alludes to Paul's Letter to Philemon and draws analogies between his own situation and that of Onesimus, the slave, and the apostle Paul. Ignatius even plays on the name Onesimus. There appear to be only two real possibilities: (a) Onesimus, the bishop of Ephesus, either was none other than the slave, Onesimus, concerning whom Paul wrote his Epistle to Philemon, or (b) he is a namesake of that Onesimus, whom Ignatius saw fit to associate by allusion with the Onesimus of the Epistle to Philemon. In either case, there is some significant connection between the bishop of Ephesus and the Onesimus referred to in Paul's Letter to Philemon.

(2) A slave who, through the apostolic ministry of Paul, had been brought into the service of Christ, and had risen to a role of leadership in the Church, would have understood very well the powerful influence of Paul as a letter writer, and would have had a worthy motive to undertake the collection, and just grounds for insisting that local Churches provide copies of any letters from Paul that might be in their custody.

(3) Certainly a bishop of Ephesus would have had the resources in terms of assistants, finances, and influence to see that the collection, whoever actually made it, was properly edited and published. That is, he could have arranged for edited copies of it to be made and circulated in other Churches.

(4) The best evidence available makes it clear that the Epistle to Philemon was the only personal letter included in the original collection of Paul's letters. This original list included the Epistle to the Ephesians which is often regarded as deutero-Pauline. So, the collection could presumably have included one or more of the Pastoral Epistles. These, like Philemon, were addressed to individuals, not churches. Therefore, the presence of the little personal letter to Philemon, in the original collection of Paul's letters, is remarkable, and is best explained if someone who had a vital interest in that little personal letter also had a decisive influence in deciding which letters of Paul were to be included in the collection. Who better than Onesimus, the former slave, might that have been? And how might such a former slave have accomplished so important a project, had he not achieved sufficient stature in the Church so that he could exert his influence in many other Churches?

It is a significant fact that Ignatius, on his way to martyrdom in

Rome, met Onesimus, bishop of Ephesus in Smyrna. It is no less significant that the young bishop of Smyrna, Polycarp, was their episcopal host. Bishops of other Asian churches were present, as well. But Onesimus, Ignatius and Polycarp would have been the pillars. So far as is known, there had not been a gathering of bishops since the apostolic council in Jerusalem as important as this meeting in Smyrna. After this meeting, the canon of Scriptures of the anti-Gnostic Church would henceforth always include (1) the corpus of Paul's letters, including Ephesians, and (2) those Gospels which featured the flesh and blood existence of Jesus and the physical reality of his passion.

When scholars reconstruct the original list of the published collection of Paul's letters, Ephesians stands first, while Galatians comes after Thessalonians and before Colossians.[84] Marcion chose to place Galatians first and to replace Galatians with Ephesians. All students of Marcion think that he did this for theological reasons. Could there have been another reason as well? Is there anything in the text of Galatians that could justify displacing, from first place, a book like Ephesians which, all would agree, is well suited to introduce the Pauline corpus whether or not, as Goodspeed thought, it was composed for that purpose?

b. Galatians 6:14–16

Does the word "canon" occur within the New Testament itself? If it does, is it ever used in a way that could have actually influenced the formation of the New Testament canon? The answer to both of these questions is yes. The word "canon" is found, interestingly enough, in Paul's Epistle to the Galatians. And, even more interesting, it is used there in a way that may have profoundly influenced the formation of the New Testament canon.

In the closing section of this, perhaps his most powerful and influential letter, Paul wrote as follows:

> Far be it from me to glory except in the cross of our Lord, Jesus Christ, by which the world has been crucified to me, and I to the world. For, neither circumcision counts for anything, nor uncircumcision, but a new creation (6:14–15).

The words that follow immediately may be translated (and are generally so translated): "Peace and mercy be upon all who walk by this 'canon,' upon the Israel of God." This may well have been close to what Paul meant to say. But it should be remembered that this is the letter in which Paul in his frustration cries out, "Would to God they would castrate themselves!" In any case, Marcion wanted to read Paul in ways that would support his conviction that Christians follow a different path than that trod by the Jews. Christians worship the loving Father of Jesus Christ. The Jews worship the just Creator God of Israel.

Galatians 6:16 can be read to mean: "Peace be upon all who walk by this 'canon' (the cross of our Lord, Jesus Christ), and mercy be upon the Israel of God."[85]

Granting Marcion's basic theological dualism, there is no reason to doubt that this is how he would have read this text. This is not to suggest that Marcion would have rightly understood Paul if by so reading this text he understood Paul to mean that Christians should reject the Scriptures of Israel. But Paul would certainly have understood the "cross of our Lord, Jesus Christ" as the absolute measure by which Christians should walk. We can certainly say this: a Marcionite reading of Paul in this passage would result in the following understanding: "The cross of our Lord, Jesus Christ" is the "canon" by which Christians should be guided. Those who walk by *this* canon will be blessed with peace. As for the "Israel of God," i.e., those who walk by the "canon" of Moses, "may mercy be upon them." Those who insist on following the "canon" of the Mosaic law and insist on circumcision condemn themselves. The most they can expect is mercy. They cannot expect peace. Their search for Shalom is void and empty! Their temple is no more. Their city is in ruins. And they have brought it upon themselves.

From this point of view, the idea of a *new* "canon" in distinction from the "canon" of the Jewish Scriptures would be quite natural. And it would lead right on to the kind of "canon" Marcion eventually developed for his Churches, *with Paul's Letter to the Galatians at the head of the "apostle."*

In this way, with Paul's letters and Marcion's Gospel free from all corrupting interpolations (just as the Alexandrian grammarians had had to free Homer and Plato from corrupting interpolations before they published their edited texts), Christians would indeed have "an absolute standard of pure language," an "absolute standard" which "one should use for the proof of doctrine."

It must be emphasized that, so far as we know, Marcion never made explicit use of Galatians 6:16. If, in fact, he made no use of this passage, it would suggest that the word "canon" in and of itself held little interest for Marcion. Apart from the presence of the word "canon" in this passage, Galatians 6:14–16 is undistinguished, it being but a part of a summary of the overall argument of Galatians. For Marcion to move Galatians itself to the head of his "apostle" is to make the strongest possible statement about what he thought should be normative for Christians.

10. 2 PETER

a. 2 Peter and the New Testament Canon

2 Peter is distinctive in certain respects which are important for understanding the development of the New Testament canon. The author writes:

> Simon Peter, a servant and apostle of Jesus Christ (1:1). . . . This is now the second letter that I have written to you . . . that you should remember the predictions of the holy prophets and the commandment of the Lord and Savior through your apostles (3:1–2).

It has been concluded from these words that the author of this Epistle knew 1 Peter and that he wrote from a viewpoint from which he could look back to the time of the apostles. He asked his readers to *remember* what had come to them from the apostles.

The author recognized the value of "gnosis" but he wanted his readers to be surrounded by other virtues, like self-discipline and brotherly affection. He writes:

> Make every effort to supplement your faith with virtue, and virtue with knowledge, and knowledge with self-control, and self-control with steadfastness, and steadfastness with

godliness, and godliness with brotherly affection, and brotherly affection with love (1:5–7).

He warned against Gnostic myths and endorsed the apostolic accounts in the Gospels:

> We did not follow cleverly devised myths when we made known to you the power and coming of our Lord Jesus Christ, but we were eyewitnesses of his majesty. For, when he received honor and glory from God the Father and the voice was borne to him by the majestic glory, 'This is my beloved Son, with whom I am well pleased,' we heard this voice borne from heaven, for we were with him on the holy mountain. And we have the prophetic word made more sure. You will do well to pay attention to this as to a lamp shining in a dark place, until the day dawns and the morning star rises in your hearts. First of all, you must understand this: that no prophecy of Scripture is a matter of one's own interpretation, because no prophecy ever came by the impulse of man, but man moved by the Holy Spirit spoke from God (1:16–21).

A close comparison of the text of this Epistle with the story of the transfiguration in the Gospels (Mt 17:1–8; Mk 9:2–8; Lk 9:28–36) indicates that the author has before him a copy of the text of the Gospel of Matthew. He is looking out upon a new world of Christian writings in which there are many Gnostic books containing what he discounts as "cleverly devised myths." And as for what the Christian Gnostics call "myths" in the Gospels, these are something quite different. The Gospels give us eyewitness testimony from apostles who were in the closest possible relationship to Jesus. These apostles were allowed to see the glory of Jesus Christ on the holy mountain where Jesus was transfigured before their very eyes.

The best way to interpret the prophecies of the Scriptures is to depend upon the Holy Spirit which, after all, moved the men who made the prophecies in the first place. He continues his warning:

False prophets also arose among the people, just as there will be false teachers among you who will secretly bring in destructive heresies . . . (2:1).

Having warned his readers against these false teachers, who are promoters of the heresies based on the books containing "cleverly devised myths," the author of 2 Peter reminds them that there is judgment in store for those who follow these false teachers, but hope for those who are faithful and righteous:

. . . God did not spare the ancient world, but preserved Noah. . . . He condemned Sodom and Gomorrah . . . and rescued Lot (2:4–8).

Clearly our author expects his readers to know and accept the Old Testament Scriptures. Later he assumes that they know the story from the Book of Numbers about Balaam's ass (2:16).

At the end of his letter, the author of 2 Peter acknowledges the difficulties that are created in the Church when Paul's letters are abused and the apostle Paul is set over against the other apostles:

Count the forbearance of our Lord as salvation. So, also, our beloved brother Paul wrote to you according to the wisdom given him, speaking of this as he does in all his letters. There are some things in them hard to understand, which the ignorant and unstable twist to their own destruction, as they do the other Scriptures . . . (3:15–16).

It is clear that the author of 2 Peter lives at a time and place where there is a consciousness in the Church of the need to emphasize that the apostles Peter, James and John are in fundamental solidarity with their blessed brother Paul, whose letters bear witness to the wisdom of God, but are being twisted by those who do not understand them correctly. These people, like the false teachers espousing their "gnosis" based on "cleverly devised myths," are doomed to destruction. They also twist to their own destruction the "other Scriptures," by which term the author of 2 Peter presumably refers to the Gospels, as well as the Old Testament writings.

There are four elements of the Christian canon of Scripture present in 2 Peter. First, the Old Testament is a source for revelation or knowledge of how God has acted and therefore will act. Possibly it is also a source of prophecy. Second, at least the Gospel of Matthew is known and is perceived to contain apostolic testimony to the revelation of God in Jesus Christ. Presumably, it also is perceived to provide apostolic witness to "the Commandments of the Lord." Thus, there is a clear appeal to *Gospel tradition.* Third, Paul's letters are recognized as having the status of Scripture, and are appealed to as providing authoritative doctrinal texts. Fourth, there is appeal to *apostolic authority,* and possibly to the authority of Christian prophets.

There is evidence that the author of 2 Peter made use of the Epistle of Jude. If this is true, a remarkable state of affairs now becomes clear: the author of what may be one of the latest books of the New Testament knows or refers to the letters of Paul; the First Epistle of Peter makes use of the Epistle of Jude, and the Gospel of Matthew, and the author identifies himself with Peter, James and John, on the Mount of Transfiguration. It cannot be an accident that these apostolic names are exactly the same as those represented in the titles given to the books of the New Testament, neither more, nor less.

Since 2 Peter is clearly a pseudonymous work, and was written at a time when the Church was in need of warning against those who composed "cleverly devised myths" (the Gnostics) and those who misinterpreted Paul (Marcion and the Gnostics), and since the author's identifiable association with apostolic names is the same as the list of apostolic names that emerged from the canon making process that can be traced back to Rome, where Marcion and the Gnostics were affecting the formation of the New Testament, it seems reasonable to conclude that this Epistle, in some conscious connection with the others that were later disputed in the Church, i.e., 2 and 3 John, James and Jude, came into the post-Marcion "Catholic" canon in Rome in the first decades of the second half of the second century, when the Church was seeking to expand the list of apostolic letters beyond the ten-letter Pauline corpus of Marcion.

b. 2 Peter and Hippolytus

According to Goodspeed, the first certain use of 2 Peter is found in the writings of Hippolytus, presbyter of Rome, who lived c. A.D. 165–235. There is also some evidence that Hippolytus knew the Epistles of James and Jude. However, a careful examination of his extant writings indicates that his normative New Testament was not significantly other than that of Irenaeus who was his teacher.[86]

Hippolytus' major work was his *Refutation of All Heresies,* which in part was based on the earlier *Against Heresies* composed by Irenaeus. Hippolytus died as a martyr during the persecution under Maximin (c. A.D. 235–239). All of this evidence from Hippolytus comports with the general conclusions to which our analysis of the problem of the development of the New Testament canon has otherwise brought us.

Persecution and martyrdom along with the threat of heresy and the Catholic response to that threat were significant factors contributing to the formation of the New Testament canon. The Gospel of Jesus Christ itself is the primary cause for the New Testament. But persecution and heresy were major secondary factors causing the Church to form the particular New Testament that has been handed down in the Church.

The main connection between the New Testament of Irenaeus in Gaul and the New Testament of Origen in Egypt was the Church in Rome. *It was in Rome during the life-span of Irenaeus, Hippolytus and Origen that the creative compromises were found that contributed to the Christian Bible of Origen.* However, we must not overemphasize the importance for Origen of the Church in Rome. Origen reminds us of the importance of persecution and martyrdom in forming the character of the Church in Alexandria. Seven years after the martyrdom of Hippolytus, Origen, looking back forty years to the persecutions that took his father and some of his friends, wrote as follows:

> This was when one really was a believer, when one used to go to martyrdom with courage in the Church, when returning from the cemeteries whither we had accompanied the bodies of the martyrs, we came back to our meetings, and

the whole Church would be assembled there, unbreakable. Then the catechumens were catechized in the midst of the martyrdoms, and in turn, these catechumens overcame tortures and confessed the living God without fear. It was then that we saw prodigies. Then too, the faithful were few in numbers but were really faithful, advancing along "the straight and narrow path leading to life" (Mt 7:14).[87]

The role of Christian apology, the combating of heresy, the administrative wisdom of countless unknown bishops, the concept of "apostolicity," and the courage and commitment of thousands of nameless confessors and martyrs must be taken into account when we think about the development of the New Testament canon.

However, there are certain particular lines of development that have emerged from this study. These lines of development can be identified with certain key figures in Church history. In the form of an overall outline we can sketch out at least the following lines of development: (1) from Syria to Asia Minor and Rome with Ignatius; (2) from Asia Minor to Rome with Polycarp; (3) from Asia Minor to Gaul with Irenaeus; (4) from Gaul back to Rome with Irenaeus and Hippolytus; (5) from Rome to Alexandria with Hippolytus and Origen; (6) from Alexandria to Caesarea and Cappadocia with Origen; (7) from Caesarea and Alexandria to Constantinople with Eusebius and Athanasius. Rome is obviously central to this development. And at each stage in this development we are to recognize that there was a wider and wider acceptance of this developing Roman tradition until, with empire-wide persecution, the tradition itself became empire-wide. Therefore, by the time of Eusebius it could probably be said with a great deal of justification: these are the books that are accepted in the Church everywhere.

NOTES

1. In modern translations of the New Testament prepared for use in Syrian Orthodox Churches in India, all these books have been given a place, for ecumenical reasons, although the authorities in these Churches would never agree that their briefer official canon is "deficient." In fact, they realize that their briefer twenty-two book canon is closer to the "undisputed" list of New Testament books acknowledged in the pre-Constantinian period than is the twenty-seven book canon of the post-Constantinian Chalcedonian Churches.

2. Festal Epistle 39, 363 A.D. Migne, *PG* 26.1437.

3. I am endebted to Bruce Metzger for drawing my attention to the substantial manuscript support for placing the Catholic epistles before the epistles of Paul. Except for the fourth century Sinaiticus which places Paul's Epistles immediately after the four Gospels and places Acts between Paul's Epistles and the Catholic Epistles, all uncials which have both Paul's Epistles and the Catholic Epistles place the Catholic Epistles before Paul's Epistles. Cf. William Hatch, *The Principal Uncial Manuscripts of the New Testament* (Chicago: University of Chicago Press, 1939). How this strongly attested tradition for ordering the Catholic Epistles before Paul's Epistles could eventually have been reversed so that Paul's Epistles come before the Catholic Epistles in our received New Testament remains, at present, unexplained.

4. C. P. Gregory, *Canon and Text of the New Testament* (New York: Scribner's, 1924) 275–277.

5. Eusebius, *E.H.* 3.25.1–7.

6. Eusebius, *E.H.* 3.31.6.

7. E. J. Goodspeed, *The Formation of the New Testament* (Chicago: University of Chicago Press, 1926) 332–335.

8. See footnote 3.

9. In *Jesus and the Gospel* (Philadelphia: Fortress Press, 1981), I argue in detail that Constantine's concern for doctrinal unity contributed to the closing of the canon. Since Eusebius is alone before Amphilochus in arranging Paul before the Catholic Epistles, only an influence of great magnitude could account for this arrangement prevailing. Eusebius' connection with

Constantine opened the door to such influence, and Constantine's commission to Eusebius to arrange for the production of fifty copies of the Bible for his new Churches in Constantinople would have occasioned the possibility for a uniform number and a uniform arrangement to be set, which uniformity could have constituted the "influence of great magnitude."

10. *Alexandrian Christianity*, The Library of Christian Classics (Philadelphia: Westminster Press, 1954) 391.

11. *Loc. cit.*

12. R.M. Grant, *The Formation of the New Testament* (New York: Harper and Row, 1965), 175.

13. W.H.C. Frend, *Martyrdom and Persecution in the Early Church* (Oxford: Clarendon, 1965); cf. Klaus Koschorke, *Die Polemik der Gnostiker Gegen das Kirchliche Christentum* (Leiden: Brill, 1978). See especially Koschorke's discussion of this problem in his section on "Das nichtige Zeugnis der Kirchlichen Märtyrer," 127–34, and his "Exkurs V: Gnosis and Martyrium," 134–137.

14. Goodspeed, *Formation* 89.

15. Cf. *Stromata*, 6. Clement justified by scriptural and philosophical argument the ideal of what he termed "the Gnostic martyr." But Clement's views, if followed, would seldom, if ever, lead Christians to engage the civil authorities. Clement never envisioned the peculiar call for martyrdom set by the Edict of Septimius Severus.

16. Eusebius reports about Origen: "His name became celebrated among the leaders in the faith, through the kindness and good will which he manifested toward all holy martyrs, whether known to him, or strangers. For not only was he with them while in bonds, and until their final condemnation, but when the holy martyrs were led to death, he was very bold and went with them into danger. So that as he acted bravely, and with great boldness saluted the martyrs with a kiss, oftentimes the heathen multitude round about them became infuriated, and were on the point of rushing on him." *E.H.* 6.3.3–4.

17. Cf. Otto Stählin, L. Früchtel, eds., *Clemens Alexandrinus* (GCS 12, 15, 17, 39; Leipzig: Hinrichs, 1905–1960); J. Ruwet, "Clement d'Alexandrie, Canon des écritures et apocryphes," *Biblica* 29 (1948) 240–271. I am especially indebted in this section to the observations made by Goodspeed, *Formation* 81–88, Grant, *Formation* 162–169, and James A. Brooks, "Clement of Alexandria as a Witness to the Development of the New Testament Canon," an unpublished research paper presented to the Southwest Seminar on the Development of Catholic Christianity, meeting at the University of Dallas, October 1980.

18. *Clemens Alexandrinus*, 4 (GCS 39) 1–59.

19. Goodspeed, *Formation* 88.

20. In making this summary, in addition to the essential information that can be gleaned from Eusebius, *E.H.* 6.25, Goodspeed, *Formation* 89–97, and Grant, *Formation* 169–175, a basic work is that of J. Ruwet, "Les 'Antilegomena dans les oeuvres d'Origenes (I)," *Biblica*, 23 (1942) 18–42; (II), 24 (1943) 18–58.

21. Goodspeed, *Formation* 93–94.

22. *Lives of Illustrious Men* (61), *Nicene and Post-Nicene Fathers*, 3 (Grand Rapids: Eerdmans) 375.

23. Goodspeed, *Formation* 95.

24. *Ibid.*

25. Hippolytus knew other books which he did not accept: *The Revelation of Peter*, *The Acts of Paul*, 2 Peter, James and Jude, and *The Shepherd of Hermas*. Cf. Goodspeed, *Formation* 95–96.

26. *Ibid.*, 96.

27. *Ibid.*, 97.

28. *Ibid.*

29. "A fifth influence on Christian Alexandria was Irenaeus." Walter J. Burghardt, "Free Like God: Recapturing an Ancient Anthropology," *Theology Digest*, 26 (1978) 348.

30. Rowan A. Greer, *Origen: An Exhortation to Martyrdom, Prayer, First Principles: Book IV, Prologue to the Commentary on the Song of Songs, Homily 27 on Numbers* (New York: Paulist Press, 1979) 1.

31. Greer, *Origen* 2.

32. *Stromata* 1.1.

33. *Stromata* 4.4.

34. *Stromata* 4.6. See Elaine Pagels, *The Gnostic Paul, Gnostic Exegesis of the Pauline Letters* (Philadelphia: Fortress Press, 1975), for the Gnostic use of Paul.

35. *Exhortation to Martyrdom* 13.

36. *Ibid.* 37. Cf. Rowan A. Greer, *The Captain of Our Salvation: A Study of the Patristic Exegesis of Hebrews* (Tübingen: Mohr, 1973) 253–254.

37. *Exhortation to Martyrdom* 36.

38. *Alexandrian Christianity* 391.

39. Adolf von Harnack, *The Origin of the New Testament*, translated by J.R. Wilkinson (London: Williams and Norgate, 1925) 169–178. Although Harnack refers to these seven starting points as "embryonic collections," they are in fact hypothetical constructs standing for collections that conceivably could have developed. Cf. Helmut Köster, "One Jesus and Four Primitive Gospels," *Trajectories Through Early Christianity* (Philadelphia: Fortress, 1971) 158–204.

40. Cf. the introduction by J.M. Robinson to *The Nag Hammadi Library in English* (San Francisco: Harper and Row, 1977) 1–21.

41. *E.H.* 6.12.3–6.

42. Note that the question of "apostolicity" is being determined by conformity to an accepted notion known as "the true faith," not by appeal to evidence concerning authorship. If Peter or Paul had ever written a book which deviated from this norm it would not be "apostolic." (Cf. Gal 1:8–9.)

43. See Frend, *Martyrdom*.

44. *E.H.* 5, preface.

45. The imagery here is probably to be associated with the Roman notion of "devotio." See Walter Burkert, *Structure and History in Greek Mythology and Ritual* (Berkeley: Univ. of Calif., 1979), 63, for a discussion and for reference to primary sources.

46. Eusebius, *E.H.* 5.4.1–2.

47. *E.H.* 5.1.17–20.

48. *E.H.* 5.2.4–5.

49. *E.H.* 5.2.6–7.

50. *E.H.* 5.2.8.

51. How particular it is may be seen by comparing it with the Scriptures that had a part in the formation of the Christian martyrs of North Africa where the fourfold Gospel and the Pauline corpus are less important, and books like the Similitudes of Enoch, Hermas and the Apocalypse of Peter are of special influence. Cf. W.H. Frend, *Martyrdom* 363.

52. *E.H.* 5.3.4.

53. E. Pagels, "Gnostic and Orthodox Views of Christ's Passion: Paradigms for the Christian's Response to Persecution?" *The Rediscovery of Gnosticism: Proceedings of the International Conference on Gnosticism at Yale, New Haven, Connecticut, March 28–31, 1978* (Studies in the History of Religions 41; ed. B. Layton; Leiden: Brill, 1980) 1. 262–283. Cf. W.H.C. Frend, *The Early Church* (Philadelphia: Lippincott, 1966) 65: "The Gnostic was not a man of martyrdom. Indeed, he deliberately rejected its necessity. . . ."

54. So Pagels concludes rightly. Cf. Frend (The *Early Church* 65): "There was to be no 'Witness Against the World.' " This also helps explain the Gnostics' need for and use of Gospels which do not feature the flesh and blood martyrdom of Jesus.

55. Hans von Campenhausen, *The Formation of the Christian Bible* (Philadelphia: Fortress Press, 1972) 207.

56. My reading of the evidence is supportive of the conclusion of Kenneth L. Carroll that the role of Montanism in the creation of the New Testament was not as decisive as Goodspeed and others have held. I do not

agree, however, that Knox has overemphasized the influence of the Marcionite movement. And I see no reason to follow Carroll in challenging Knox's judgment that the "New Testament came into existence as a conscious creation between 150 and 175, which was probably the period of Marcion's most vigorous and influential activity." (Cited by Carroll in "The Earliest New Testament," *BJRL* 38 [1955] 48–51.) I see Luke-Acts as a pre-Marcionite work. Therefore, unlike Knox, I cannot credit Marcion with creating the "Gospel-apostle" form of the New Testament. But there is no way to be sure that had Marcion not followed the "Gospel-apostle" model of Luke-Acts in forming his New Testament, the Church would have done so. As Harnack shows, there were various shapes the New Testament might have assumed. Undoubtedly, then, the fact that Marcion followed one particular model had a decisive influence on the creation of the New Testament of the Church to the extent that the Church responded to Marcion's challenge by developing this model even further.

57. W.R. Farmer, "Modification and Creation of Tradition," in *Jesus and the Gospel* (Philadelphia: Fortress Press, 1982).

58. Alfred Resch, *Agrapha: Ausserkanonische Schriftfragmente* (TU 15, 3–4; 2nd ed. Leipzig: Hinrichs 1906; reprinted, Darmstadt: Wissenschafliche Buchgesellschaft, 1967) and H. Köster *Synoptische Überlieferung bei den apostolischen Vätern* (TU 65; Berlin: Akademie 1957).

59. Cf. Robert Funk, "The Apostolic Parousia: Form and Significance," *Christian History and Interpretation: Studies Presented to John Knox,* eds. W.R. Farmer, C.F.D. Moule, and R.R. Niebuhr (Cambridge: Cambridge U. Press, 1967) 249–268.

60. John Knox, "Acts and the Pauline Letter Corpus," *Studies in Luke-Acts,* eds. Leander E. Keck and J. Louis Martyn (Nashville: Abingdon, 1966) 279–287.

61. For evidence that Mark was written after Matthew and Luke, see Hans-Herbert Stoldt, *History and Criticism of the Marcan Hypothesis* (Macon: Mercer University Press, 1980) and William R. Farmer, "The Secondary Character of Mark," in *Jesus and the Gospel* (Philadelphia: Fortress Press, 1982).

62. J. Knox, *Marcion and the New Testament: An Essay in the Early History of the Canon* (Chicago: University of Chicago Press, 1942) 156.

63. Adolf Harnack, *Marcion: Das Evangelium von fremden Gott* (2nd ed.; Leipzig: J.C. Hinrichs, 1924, reprinted, Darmstadt: Wissenschaftliche Buchgesellschaft, 1969) 243.

64. *E.H.* 5.24.9.

65. "Er mag um das Jahr 85 oder etwas später geborn sein." Adolf von Harnack, *Marcion* 21; Frend, *Early Church* 66.

66. Cf. Robert M. Grant, *Gnosticism and Early Christianity* (New York: Columbia University Press, 1966) 122. I am indebted to David Balas for drawing my attention to Grant's discussion of this matter. What I have written was written before reading Grant. Our two accounts represent quite independent historical reconstructions. Needless to say, we could both independently be wrong in our common conjecture that there is some connection between Marcion's purpose in going to Rome and the recent events in Palestine. But if this conjecture is sound it could serve to ground future investigation of Marcion in the history of his time in new and important ways. David Balas has accepted as quite possible Grant's conjecture of a connection between Marcion's purpose and the bloody suppression of the Bar Cochba uprising in "Marcion Revisited: A 'Post Harnack' Perspective," in *Texts and Testaments: Critical Essays on the Bible and Early Church Fathers,* ed. W. Eugene March (San Antonio: Trinity University Press, 1980) 95–108. Balas concludes his discussion with this observation (p. 99): "Finally, the shaken confidence of many Jews in the confirmed goodness, omniscience, and all-powerfulness of Yahweh (incompatible as it seemed with the historical realities of the time) was taken as an admission that the god of the Old Testament was inferior to the all-good and perfect god revealed in Jesus Christ. Paradoxically, it was precisely by having accepted Jewish scriptures and history, at least to a large extent, in their contemporary Jewish interpretation that Marcion arrived at his radical dissociation of the two testaments!"

67. S.G.F. Brandon, *The Fall of Jerusalem and the Christian Church: A Study of the Effects of the Jewish Overthrow of A.D. 70 on Christianity* (London: S.P.C.K., 1957). See especially pp. 8–9 and 214–215.

68. Marcion went about "founding communities in opposition to the great Church which had cast him out": Frend, *Early Church* 67.

69. There can be no question about the conceptual kinship between the Gospel-apostle structure of Luke-Acts and the Gospel-apostle structure of Marcion's canon. The only question is which has influenced the other.

70. Some will say that neither did Paul succeed, and that only with later Paulinists has he had his day in court.

71. Goodspeed, *Formation* 50.

72. *Ibid.,* 51–52.

73. Cf. Arthur Bellinzoni, *The Sayings of Jesus in the Writings of Justin Martyr* (Supplements to *Novum Testamentum* 17; Leiden: Brill, 1967). Georg Strecker disputes the view that such a Gospel harmony was used by Justin in "Eine Evangelienharmonie bei Justin und Pseudoklemens?" *NTS* 24 (1978) 297–316.

74. Gregory (*Canon and Text* 73–75) goes so far as to refer to Polycarp

as the keystone of the arch that supports the history of the Church and the New Testament from the time of the apostles to the close of the second century.

75. J. B. Lightfoot, *The Apostolic Fathers* (London: Macmillan, 1926) 168–173.

76. E. Barnikol, *Die Entstehung der Kirche im zweiten Jahrhundert und die Zeit Marcions* (Forschungen zur Entstehung der Urchristentums der Neuen Testaments und der Kirche 8) (Kiel: Mühlau, 1933) 25–30.

77. Victor, bishop of Rome, had excommunicated the Churches of Asia Minor because they refused to follow those Churches in communion with the Church in Rome in the observance of Easter. Irenaeus argued against this and appealed to Victor to follow the tradition of his predecessor, Anicetus, who had shared the Eucharist with Polycarp even though agreement had not been reached on the observance of Easter. Casper Rene Gregory has noted that for Irenaeus, in addition to Marcion, who held to one Gospel and rejected all others, there was another group that held to Matthew, Mark and Luke and rejected John. Gregory proposes that those who rejected John were those a later writer, Epiphanius, called Alogians. But in view of Victor's excommunication of the Churches of Asia Minor for whom John was the most important Gospel, it seems likely that there was an influential party in Rome that adhered to the Gospels of Matthew, Mark, and Luke, and because John differed from these Gospels so widely, as for example on the date of the death of Jesus, and thus the date of Easter, they rejected that Gospel. The triumph of Irenaeus' view over that of Victor had the effect of establishing the fourfold Gospel canon once and for all in the Catholic Church. On this view the work begun by Polycarp and Anicetus was challenged by Victor, championed by Irenaeus, and eventually established by theologians and bishops who followed Irenaeus—men like Hippolytus, Origen and Eusebius. For Gregory's views *see Canon and Text* 151.

78. Cf. J.M. Robinson, ed., *The Nag Hammadi Library in English* (San Francisco: Harper and Row, 1977).

79. Robert Grant, (*Formation* 121–130) discusses the New Testament books used by Basilides and the students of Valentinus. See also E.H. Pagels, *The Gnostic Paul.*

80. According to Tertullian, Valentinus was thwarted in an attempt to become bishop (*Adv. Valent.* 4). Cf. E.H. Pagels, "Gnosticism," *The Interpreter's Dictionary of the Bible,* supplementary volume, eds. K. Crim, L.R. Bailey, Sr. and V.P. Furnish (Nashville: Abingdon, 1976) 366.

81. Frend, *Early Church* 77.

82. *Ibid.,* 70–71. This dating for Polycarp's martyrdom relies on Eusebius (4.15.1), who records Polycarp's death in the reign of Marcus Aurelius

(161–180). Other scholars relying on *Martyrdom of Polycarp* (21) place this martyrdom under the Proconsul Statius Quadratus and date it in 155. Cf. "Polycarp, St.," *New Catholic Encyclopedia,* 9.535. Still others argue for a date of February 22, 156. Cf. Kirsopp Lake, "The Martyrdom of Polycarp," *Apostolic Fathers* (Loeb Classical Library) (London: Heinemann, 1913) 2.310–311.

83. John Knox, building in part on the work of his teacher, Edgar Goodspeed and others, has gone further than anyone else in offering a credible account of the collection of Paul's letters. It is a story that involves brilliant historical conjecture combined with precise literary and exegetical analysis of both Paul's letters and the letters of Ignatius. Cf. "The Pauline Corpus" in *Marcion and the New Testament: An Essay in the Early History of the Canon* (Chicago: The University of Chicago Press, 1942) 39–76; and *Philemon Among the Letters of Paul* (Knoxville: Abingdon, 1935, revised edition, 1959) 71–108. Students of the problem of the New Testament canon will have noted that I have not followed John Knox in dating the completed work Luke-Acts after Marcion. The reason for this is that Knox presupposes Marcan priority at essential points in reaching this conclusion. Since I remain doubtful about this assumption, I must remain skeptical of Knox's results at this point. For those who accept Marcan priority, however, the critical discussion remains largely where Knox left it in 1942, in *Marcion and the New Testament.* I believe that both E.C. Blackman in *Marcion and His Influence* and Hans von Campenhausen in *The Formation of the Christian Bible* are correct in not following Knox at this point. However, neither has answered Knox's arguments and evidence, and thus their own work, which presupposes, with Knox, Marcan priority, is, at this point, critically less consistent than that of Knox. Others will have noted that I have rested nothing on the *Muratorian Canon.* The reason for this is that its date and provenance have both been thrown into doubt by Albert C. Sundberg, Jr., in "Canon Muratori: A Fourth Century List," 1–41. Sundberg's conclusions have in part been challenged by Everett Ferguson, "Canon Muratori: Date and Provenance," unpublished paper read at *Eighth International Conference on Patristic Studies,* Oxford, Sept. 3–8, 1979; to be published in *Studia Patristica* (Berlin: Akademie-Verlag).

84. John Knox, *Philemon Among the Letters of Paul,* 89.

85. Cf. E. DeW. Burton, *A Critical and Exegetical Commentary on The Epistle to the Galatians* (Edinburgh: T. and T. Clark, 1921) 357–359. Burton translates as follows: "And as many as shall walk by this rule, peace be upon them, and mercy upon the Israel of God." Burton notes that the order "peace and mercy" is illogical if both words have reference to one class of persons, since that would place effect first and cause afterward. Where these

two words are joined elsewhere in benedictions in the New Testament "mercy" always precedes "peace." So also, in the often repeated benediction "grace and peace," in which grace closely corresponds to mercy in meaning, grace always precedes peace. It is best, therefore, to take the reversal of this normal order into account and recognize that "peace" refers to those who walk by the spirit (Gal 5:25) which results in a new creation (Gal 6:15) and which comes to focus for Paul in the cross of our Lord, Jesus Christ (Gal 6:14); and "mercy" refers to the Israel of God as the Jewish nation or some part thereof. Burton considers Paul's usage of "the Israel of God" where it might refer to all believers in Christ, regardless of nationality (Rom 2:29, Phil 3:3), but concludes that in Gal 6:16 the benediction falls into two distinct parts and that Paul means to call for mercy upon Jews, not the whole Jewish nation, but pious Israel, "including even those who had not seen the truth as Paul saw it." Hans Dieter Betz does not discuss Burton's exegesis. His own solution to the problematic grammar of Paul's text is to understand Paul's usage of the term "Israel of God" in this instance to mean that Paul extends the blessing "beyond the Galatian Paulinists to those Jewish-Christians who approve of his rule in v. 15": *Galatians* (Hermeneia; Philadelphia: Fortress Press, 1979) 321–323. For our purpose, however, the point is not how Paul should be read, but how Paul could have been read. And Burton reads Paul in a way similar to how we conjecture Marcion did.

86. See above, "The New Testament Canon of Hippolytus," 16–19.

87. Frend in *Martyrdom* 322, from *Homil. in Jerem.,* 4.3.

THE EARLY DEVELOPMENT
OF THE NEW TESTAMENT CANON

by
Denis Farkasfalvy, O. Cist.

A. *Formulating the Question and Clarifying the Methodology*

From the earliest stages of its history, the Church expressed its belief in a set of sacred books, some of them identical with the sacred writings of Judaism, some of them being the product of early Christian literature. Listings of the Church's sacred books may only have been available by the end of the second century,[1] yet it is commonly accepted among historians that by that time the idea of a collection of authoritative books, considered as Holy Scripture, i.e., the idea of a Christian canon, had appeared and that actual booklists had been made. Not much objection can be raised against marking the works of Irenaeus of Lyons as the *terminus ad quem* for the early phase of the development of the canon.[2] With few exceptions and some hesitation, he used the same books and the same basic method of exegesis that characterized the giant of scriptural scholarship in the third century, Origen,[3] and after him the rest of the patristic era in both the East and the West. Our question, therefore, can be put into the following simplified terms: How did the canon and the exegetical method of Irenaeus come about?

The problem is, however, not so simple. Irenaeus does not speak of a canon as such and gives little or no historical or theological account of its development. He testifies to the beliefs of his Church that it is clearly aware of being in possession of inspired and normative books. He turns to the use and interpretation of these books whenever a theological question is raised. His claims and attitudes concerning the sacred writings of Christianity are, furthermore, in no way isolated from the rest of the Church. As Pierre Grelot has pointed out, in spite of variations of detail, substantial agreement appears among the leading figures of the Church at the beginning of the third century: Irenaeus with his ties to Asia Minor and yet bishop of Lyons in Gaul, Hippolytus in Rome, Tertullian in Latin Africa and Clement of Alexandria in Egypt virtually represent the whole geographic spread of Christianity. They use basically the same Scriptures with basically identical exegetical practices and premises.[4] Thus Irenaeus does not offer in this respect a personal synthesis but expresses a position common to the widespread network of Christian Churches, united, as it seems, in their anti-Gnostic position. Our task is, therefore, to trace the path of development that led to this position which we encounter in all major centers of Christianity.

Nevertheless, it would be tempting to reformulate our question and assign to it some rather simple terms. After all, Christianity took its origin in the realm of Judaism, a religion firmly holding to the possession of sacred books. Even if the exact and definitive list of the Jewish canon was drawn up only at or after its split with Christianity, one might still say that the belief in Sacred Scriptures belongs to "the Jewish bag" that the Church has carried with itself since its earliest origins. The question is only this: How did it come to the idea of including among the sacred writings books of its own making? When, why and how did the Church decide to include some of its own early literature as Scripture alongside the books inherited from Judaism, by thus extending the concept of inspired and normative writings also to these products of Christian literary activities? This rather "simple" way of formulating our question is quite frequent in scholarly literature about the canon. Following a preconceived evolutionary path, numerous authors have tried to reconstruct the successive development by which the concept of *graphe* was step-by-step extended to the early and venerable accounts of Jesus, the letters of Paul and a number of other writings, correctly or incorrectly attributed to some important figures of the early Church.[5] This approach usually supposes that the development of the New Testament canon was gradual and that it took place by the extension of the ideas connected with the books of the Old Testament to a new set of writings. According to this supposition, the canon "emerged" gradually rather than being the product of a few innovative decisions that could be located in space and time. Furthermore, this approach excludes, on methodological grounds, the possibility that the canon of the New Testament or the Christian canon of Scriptures in general could have *meant* in the course of history something radically new, not known in earlier times. It never asks the question why the concept of "Scriptures" became susceptible of extension and hence capable of an addition of a new set of writings. It cannot explain why the Church became within a short period of time the possessor of more than twenty books of new "Holy Scripture," while it had shown no interest to do such a thing for almost two generations. This lack is more noteworthy if we realize that a "natural growth" of the canon is contrary to what happened to the Jewish Bible during the same period of time. When receiving its final shape at the end of the first century, the Jewish canon was narrowed down to those writings about which no doubts were raised, while the Christian Church expanded its holdings of sacred books and kept a more open mind about the Jewish Scriptures as well. There must be, therefore, a radical difference in their respective understanding of what Scripture is or should be. For these reasons the development of the Christian canon cannot be sufficiently explained without first finding specific causes that show why Christianity and rabbinic Judaism have taken steps in rather opposite directions.[6]

These reflections justify the perspective taken by some of the scholars dissatisfied with the concept of an "emerging canon." They are asking the question: Why, when and how did the Church come to the conclusion that the Scriptures inherited from Judaism were *incomplete,* so that a selection of Christian books should also be elevated to the status of Holy Scripture? Their point of departure is the realization that through the first hundred years of her history, the Church was unaware of Holy Scriptures other than the Old Testament. They posit, therefore, the beginnings of the New Testament canon as a change occurring in the Church sometime in the middle of the second century. Their main concern is to find the persons and causes responsible for this change. They look for the historical figure who might be credited with initiating the idea of a New Testament canon. By following Adolph Harnack's evaluation and understanding of Marcion and Marcionism, John Knox[7] and Hans von Campenhausen[8] thought that they had found the founder of the New Testament canon in this famous churchman who certainly stood in the center of attention of the anti-Gnostic Church Fathers. They came to the conclusion that the idea of a new collection of sacred writings is the logical consequence of Marcion's decision to reject Judaism and the Jewish sacred writings. A new Bible had to be created to replace the vacuum left by the Marcionite option of rejecting the law and the prophets of Judaism. This task was accomplished when Marcion canonized his Gospel (a text probably made, as Tertullian reports, by shortening and re-editing the Gospel of Luke) and a collection of ten Pauline Epistles. In this way, Marcion created a canon consisting of two parts: "Gospel" and "the apostle." The fact that this basic structure still characterizes the canon of the New Testament has been pointed to as the ultimate proof that Marcion's initiative was of decisive importance, influencing the rest of the history of the canon. All that the anti-Gnostic Church did was to extend the "Gospel" to include four accounts (a "tetramorphous" Gospel, rather than one single narration) and a larger selection of apostolic letters including works attributed not only to Paul but also to Peter, John, James and possibly others. In this perspective, of course, the Christian canon of the New Testament appears as an anti-Marcionite product which one might admire for its ecumenical broadness or deplore because of its heterogenous theological content.

This scheme that credits Marcion with inventing the idea of a New Testament is enticing for a number of reasons. Not only does it coordinate a large number of known facts of the second century history of the Church but it also provides theological interpretation for what has happened. First of all, it exalts Marcion's "Paulinism" as the fertile ground from which the idea of Christian Scriptures sprang up. In this way it attributes to the authentic Pauline letters a position of first-ranking importance within the canon. Furthermore, it detects in Marcion an attitude curiously resembling that of the Reformers of the sixteenth century and identifies this attitude with the moving force that created the New Testament canon: an attitude of uncompromising search for the authentic, original sources of Christian faith, discovered with the help of the Pauline letters. For this attitude Marcion receives admiration: in spite of his factual errors, he is a champion of authenticity who, if necessary, sides with Paul against the rest of the apostles and goes into heresy for the sake of holding high the original and unadulterated version of Christian truth. Knox explicitly states the parallelism between him and Luther, while von Campenhausen sees in him a critical mind distrusting interpolated documents and distinguishing the different layers of accumulated tradition. Needless to say, this is an idealized picture of Marcion. With a rather naive and uncritical approach it makes Marcion appear endowed with concern and skills for source criticism. Equally deceptive is the picture of the "emerging Catholic Church" pulling together under its umbrella of ecumenism a wide range of heterogeneous traditions and so creating the orthodox canon of the New Testament. In fact, further reflection and research raise suspicions that the Marcionite explanation of the origins of the canon might be incorrect, for it poorly matches some well-established facts of the Marcionite conflict. First of all, it does not explain why Marcion, when rejecting the Old Testament, started to replace it by writings that, even in their re-edited and interpolated form, showed too much connection with the Old Testament and contained more or less explicit recognition thereof. Marcion's Scripture suits his purpose so poorly that it is hardly believable that its origins are adequately explained by reference to this purpose. We see, in fact, how easily Tertullian runs through the texts of the Marcionite Bible and discovers in them a multitude of references confirming the validity of the Old Testament. Furthermore, what Marcion does with Paul supposes that he takes up his position *within* a tradition which recognizes the binding character of the apostolic authority. In fact, his use of Galatians which reports about the conflicts between Peter and Paul and anchors Paul's apostolic authority in a direct divine call cannot be explained unless Marcion confronts a Church conscious of its apostolic foundations. As we will see, this supposition is borne out by a number of texts that must be dated earlier than Marcion. In this perspective, the "Paulinism" of Marcion needs reinterpretation. When he chooses one apostle and sets him up against the others,[9] he restricts the normative base of the Church, a fact incompatible with the supposition that the creation of such a normative scriptural base was his invention.

The above considerations recommend a method cautious and

circumspect enough to give a more plausible account of all aspects of the earliest phases of the history of the Church, both those that suggest the model of an "emerging" canon and those that point to major and sudden developments taking place in the middle of the second century. We have to be aware also of the fact that the concept of a "canon of Scriptures" is composed of several notions of which some might appear earlier while others "emerge" at a later time. Canon implies normativity. The existence of normative *writings* supposes considerable spread and use of those early Christian documents. A conscious and purposeful compilation of a canon in the form of a list of books supposes reflection on the *written form* of the norm of faith while the list itself would normally serve the practical purpose of defending certain books or defending the Church *against* certain other books. All these aspects of the canon are not necessarily present at the same time; we might be able to detect different "embryonic" forms of a scriptural canon at some early stage of history. Consequently, it seems to me that one must make every attempt not to reduce the development of the canon to any linear (one-dimensional) pattern, but to look for a multiplicity of causes and factors which all together tell the whole story.

As the starting point of the investigation, it is most important to examine the role and function of the Old Testament at the beginning of the Church's life. We must first of all ascertain in what sense the early Church has "taken over" the Holy Scriptures of Israel and see if there was, right at the beginning, any room for further Scriptures or even some definite need that had to lead, with time, to the point of adopting additional Sacred Scriptures. By asking such questions first, we will detect in the way Christianity possessed Jewish Holy Scriptures an original openness to further growth. After this we shall investigate the process by which the "euaggelion"—the apostolic kerygma, held as supreme norm of faith for the Church at its birth— found expression in a multiplicity of literary products.[10] As we examine the use and spread of these documents in the early Church we shall see close ties between the development of the canon and the formation of the Church's self-understanding as an historical entity and as dependent on its beginnings. *In fact, the development of the canon coincides for the Church with its coming to terms with its own past as the norm of its future, the process of forming its consciousness of historicality.*

This conception of the problem of the canon in the early Church has thus the merit of showing the roots of the theological antithesis "Scripture—tradition." In an act of reflection upon itself, the Church of the second century set aside a collection of books as representing its first century of existence to serve it in preserving its own doctrinal identity for the future. In this we detect an act of self-definition which creates for all upcoming generations a dialectical relationship between the teaching organs of the Church (called *magisterium* in today's Roman Catholic vocabulary), functioning with authority when proposing norms of faith, and Scriptures that are to be used as the authoritative source of teaching. By investigating the origins of the canon, we can, therefore, better understand the interdependence that connects Scripture and tradition in the subsequent history of Christianity.

B. *The Role and Use of Old Testament Scriptures in the Apostolic Church*

A brief survey of the earliest available documents of the Christian faith immediately shows their essential ties with the sacred writings of Judaism. Paul's First Letter to the Corinthians, our first document testifying to the faith in the resurrection (about 55–56 A.D.), explicitly affirms this link of the Christian faith with the Scriptures of the old covenant: "For I delivered to you as of first importance what I also received, that Christ died for our sins *in accordance with the Scriptures,* that he was buried, that he was raised on the third day *in accordance with the Scriptures . . .*" (1 Cor 15:3–4). Paul is quoting here a credal formula he received from the Church[11] in which there is emphasis on the agreement between the events surrounding Christ (mainly his passion and death) and the texts of the sacred writings. It cannot be said with certainty which particular texts are meant, reference being made possibly to Hos 6:3 ("on the third day he will raise us up") or to different passages of Isaiah on the Suffering Servant. What matters for us, however, is to see that the idea of the "fulfillment of the Scriptures" appears already this early as something of fundamental importance for the Christian consciousness and the Christian proclamation.

Contrary to what our modern biblical interpretation tends to affirm, these early documents do not speak only of some "preparation" or "anticipation" of the New Testament by the Old.[12] Christian preaching in general presupposes the acceptance of the Scriptures as documents of faith, that is, authentic sources transmitting divine revelation. The general practice of the apostolic preaching to approach in every city first the Jewish communities and to extend only afterward the kerygma to the Gentiles is a living witness to this conviction.[13] And, of course, announcing Jesus to the Jews takes place in strictly scriptural terms: "He expounded the matter to them from morning till evening, testifying to the kingdom of God and trying to convince them about Jesus both from *the law of Moses and from the prophets*" (Acts 28:23). The speeches of Acts, representing a variety of strata of the apostolic preaching, bear out this summary statement. We encounter in them the same fundamental structure and logic. The point of departure is usually some biblical text from which the speaker tries to prove, with an array of supportive quotations, that Jesus is indeed the Messiah. No matter how much or how little a modern student of these texts would accept the validity of the scriptural arguments, the fact remains that from the earliest time Christian preaching has always depended on scriptural arguments and was accepted with faith because the biblical texts were deemed valid and convincing.

Our sources point even further. In the practice of the primitive Church the Scriptures are no mere tools to justify the faith of the Christians in Jesus.[14] We also encounter quite explicitly the claim that only this Christian faith can throw light on the Scriptures of the old covenant. The relationship is therefore mutual: the Scriptures prove claims about Christ and Christ is the key to understanding the Scriptures. In contemporary biblical scholarship this might appear as a vicious circle. No such problem is perceived by the apostolic generation. The mutual relationship between Christ and Scripture corresponds to their idea of Scripture as essentially *prophetic* in its entirety. For them Scripture contains and expresses a reality pregnant with promises, a reality, therefore, which becomes intelligible

only in the future. It is directed essentially toward a future fulfillment. When using scriptural proof-texts about Christ, the speaker
accomplishes a task implicit in all messianic expectations: he exhibits
events which prove and specify the messianic meaning of the texts.
Establishing correspondence between the events and the texts, he
confirms at once both the messiahship of Jesus and the messianic
purport of the texts which he quotes. Faith in Christ and faith in the
Scriptures appear as correlative and interdependent.

It is probably in the writings of Luke that the interdependence
of Christ and Scripture appears in its clearest and most conscious
form. In his Gospel, the risen Christ explains to the apostles his passion and resurrection as fulfillment of the Scriptures, that is, of the
prophecies found "in the law of Moses, the prophets and the
psalms." In this way, "he opened their minds for understanding the
Scriptures" (Lk 24:44–45). It would be false, however, to attribute
such statements to tendencies of Frühkatholizismus or to the relative
lateness of the Lukan compositions. Writings much earlier than the
Gospel of Luke express the same theology whenever the purpose and
the context of the theological theme compel the author to reflect on
the role of the ancient sacred writings. In Romans, Paul clearly affirms that he considers the Scriptures of the Jews as the legitimate
possession of the Christians; they actually fulfill the purpose for
which they had been made only when they are interpreted in the
light of Christianity. "Everything written before our time was written for our instruction" (Rom 15:4). This statement is a bold general-
ization expropriating all Scriptures for the infant Church. Should
there be any doubt about the authenticity of this passage, one might
refer to similar statements in the body of the Epistle: "The words, 'It
was credited to him' (Gen 15:6) were not written only with him
(Abraham) in view; *they were intended for us,* too" (Rom 4:23; cf
also 1 Cor 10:11).[15] 1 Peter, a document possibly coming from the
first Christian generation,[16] expresses the same claim in similar
terms. The prophets who predicted "the sufferings destined for
Christ and the glories that would follow" were quite aware that they
were providing "not for themselves but for you," and the content of
their foreknowledge is "now proclaimed to you by those who preach
the Gospel in the power of the Holy Spirit" (1 Pet 1:11–12). Thus it
seems that throughout early Christian writings behind the multiple

use of the Old Testament, there appears the firm and general conviction that the ultimate addressees of the Scriptures are "we" who received the fullness of God's revelation and accepted it with faith.[17] This belief is dramatically expressed in the Book of Revelation presenting the slaughtered and risen Lamb which opens the Book sealed with seven seals (Rev 5:1–10).[18] Christ, according to the first Christian generation, is not *some* continuation of the Old Testament; he fulfills not just *certain* of its passages. He is the true and full meaning of the Old Testament as a whole.

To what extent does the Church's claim of the Scriptures as its own go back to the words, practices and attitudes of Jesus himself? The efforts made to verify this from the Synoptic tradition[19] were halted by the uncertainties surrounding both the Synoptic question and the meager results of the repeated quests of the historical Jesus. The fact that Jesus preached in synagogues is attested by all Synoptic Gospels (Mt 4:23; 13:53; Mk 1:21; 3:1; 6:2; Lk 4:15–16). Did he indeed present himself as the fulfillment of the Scriptures as Luke has it in connection with Is 61:1–2: "Today this Scripture has been fulfilled in your hearing" (Lk 4:21)? Or is this scene only a retrojection of the apostolic preaching as conceived by Luke and described in Acts? For the purpose of this study it should be sufficient to see that each of the four Gospels understood Jesus in this way.

One might say that, with regard to the role of the Scriptures in Jesus' ministry, the four Gospels present a divergent convergency. Without any doubt, Luke is the one who is the most aware and emphatic about the Christian interpretation and understanding of Scripture as the fruit of Jesus' preaching, death and resurrection. Without necessarily accepting the subtleties of Laurentin's analysis of the infancy narratives we can see that the first two chapters have one main thrust: Jesus encompasses in himself, right at his birth, at his first arrival to Israel, all the expectations and promises of God's people.[20] This, combined with the interpretations of the Scriptures by the risen Christ quoted above (Lk 24:44–45), constitutes a true "inclusion," that is, some sort of framework making Jesus appear as the one whom all preceding kings and prophets wanted to see. Luke's remarkable expression "prophets and apostles" as messengers of God's wisdom on earth[21] may not refer to two distinct categories of divine delegates, yet it gives away his awareness that God's salvific acts are all integrated into a unified plan from the very beginning of creation up to the apostolic proclamation.

Of course, even a superficial reading of Matthew reveals the concern of the evangelist to present Jesus as the fulfillment of the Scriptures, as the one who completes and transcends the law and the prophets. It is even more important for us to see that he presents Jesus as conscious of all this, speaking as the legislator who both maintains and upgrades the standards of the old law: "You have heard that it was said. . . . But I say to you . . ." (Mt 5:21, 27, 33, 38, 43).

Mark presents probably the least amount of theological reflection on Jesus' relationship to Old Testament Scripture. It is therefore all the more significant that he maintains the basic features of Jesus' Scripture-based ministry in the synagogues by transmitting several instances in which Jesus is engaged in controversy and uses scriptural references about the meaning of his mission and message (cf. Mk 12:10–11, 36–37).

For Mark's understanding of Jesus' relationship to the Old Testament, his presentation of the parable about the wicked vinedressers is most enlightening (Mk 12:1–12). The parable appears in Mark as a theological statement about the unity and continuity of salvation history put into the form of a popular tale. In this framework, Jesus is shown to belong to a series of divine missions.[22] His coming—the coming of the Son—completes and crowns the previous sendings of different servants, the prophets of the Old Testament. The story relates both the fact that Jesus belongs to the series of the prophets who preceded him and that his coming is superior in dignity and importance to all previous messengers.

In John, the testimony of the Scriptures appears as an important theme on which the evangelist reflexively elaborates. That the truth about Jesus must be obtained by means of scriptural arguments is presupposed and remains unquestioned. His enemies argue with biblical quotations: "Is the Christ to come from Galilee? Has not the Scripture said that the Christ is descended from David and comes from Bethlehem, the village where David was?" (Jn 7:42). Similarly, Jesus himself builds his arguments on Scripture texts: "You search the Scriptures, because you think that in them you have eternal life; and it is they that bear witness to me" (Jn 5:39). Those who reject him reject Moses as well, for the acceptance of Moses would necessarily result in the acceptance of Jesus: "It is Moses who accuses you on whom you set your hope. If you believed Moses, you would believe me, for he wrote of me" (Jn 5:45–46). This strict coordination of faith in Scriptures (Moses) and faith in Jesus is, however, not a particular feature of John's Gospel. The same thought echoes in Luke: "If they do not hear Moses and the prophets (the formula clearly envisages the totality of Scriptures), neither will they be convinced if someone should rise from the dead" (Lk 16:31).

In view of the evidence quoted from our earliest Christian sources, one might be tempted to conclude that the Church "inherited," so to speak, the Scriptures of the Old Testament. Such a statement is, however, simplistic and inexact. On the one hand, it supposes that at the birth of Christianity the Scriptures of the Old Testament existed as a precisely circumscribed and identifiable collection of books. Yet, in spite of the global references to "the Scriptures" or "the law and the prophets" throughout the first century, the Jewish canon's closure did not come about before the end of that century, under circumstances which forced the Jewish community to make decisions reflecting their recent separation from those who accepted Christianity. On the other hand—and this seems to be more important—"taking over" the Scriptures of the Old Testament should not be conceived of as if Christians continued to hold the same beliefs about them and used them in the same way as Jews did previously. In spite of all the similarities in vocabulary and concepts regarding inspiration, prophecy and hermeneutical practices, belief in Christ as the fulfillment of Scriptures creates a qualitative difference between Judaism and the Church so that their relationship to the old Scriptures is no longer the same. One might even say with some simplification that starting in the second century scriptural interpretation is, in fact, the central issue in every confrontation between Christian and non-Christian Jews. Also, when accepting the same scriptural text they differ about its interpretation and ultimate salvific meaning. For Christians, all texts refer to a fulfillment realized or to be realized in Christ, the crucified and risen Jesus of Nazareth, and in his Church. Judaism on the contrary rejects Christianity and explains this decision by refusing its interpretation of the sacred writings. It is the understanding of the Scriptures that separates

Church and synagogue, and for centuries they continue arguing about their differences in the form of biblical controversy.

That the Jewish canon is in the end more restrictive than the Old Testament canon of the Christians is probably of minor importance, but it documents the same point. It is the christological use of the Scriptures that makes the Church interested in including a larger number of books, while the anti-Christian bias of the synagogue turns the Jewish authorities to conservatism and caution.

In the Christian use of the Old Testament, these Scriptures become documents of a unique and unified salvation history whose center and peak is Jesus Christ. Being used as documents to be understood fully only in reference to Christ, these writings obtain a significantly new place and function in salvation history. They are not regarded as the last proclamation of God's truth. They are superseded and transcended by later events and divine revelation. But the later word of God does not destroy the validity of the earlier ones; it only presents them with a wider context so that their ultimate purpose and truth may be made manifest.

As we have seen, in every branch of recorded Christian thinking of the apostolic age we can detect the presence of this concern to use the old Jewish texts as (a) documents proving the validity of the Christian proclamation and (b) writings which make the Church understand Christ more fully, that is, documents that can be fully understood only in the light of Christian faith. This christological perspective, we might say, relativizes the Jewish writings insofar as it subordinates them to the *euaggelion*. On the other hand, Christians think of themselves as the ones who finally have obtained the true meaning of these texts. They take them into possession with the consciousness of rightful ownership just as they declare themselves true sons of Abraham or the true Israel. In Christ, they believe, they have reached a vantage point from which they can come to the full and valid understanding of these Scriptures. This conviction makes them feel that they are the legitimate owners of the Old Testament books in an exclusive sense.

Thus, considering the Christian context of the Jewish sacred writings, one must immediately say that they do not possess the highest and exclusive normativity with respect to the Christian faith.

Although they are firmly believed to be the word of God, they are possessed with the conviction that the fullness of the Word was Jesus Christ (cf. Jn 1:1–18; Heb 1:1–4; cf. 1 Jn 1:1–2). In this perspective, "the law and the prophets"—a comprehensive expression for all Scriptures in Judaism—becomes less and less "law" and appears more and more as "prophecy." Actually, it is considered prophecy in its entirety. Of course the word of God pronounced before the coming of Christ is never considered as lessened in divine authority. Yet its normative validity is recognized only in reference to its messianic function, in virtue of the ultimate clarification brought to the old texts by the deeds and words of Christ. Such a development, already detectable in Paul, is seen later in full clarity. With the destruction of the temple and the Jewish national establishment, Christianity discounts the actual validity of the legal and ritual texts and consciously converts all texts into "prophecy" by establishing a full-scale search for transposing the content of the Old Testament into christological message. The Epistle to the Hebrews and the letter of Barnabas are probably the best illustration of this full-fledged exploitation of the Old Testament as prophecy about Christ. No wonder that at this time "the prophets" becomes more and more frequently a comprehensive expression designating all the authors of the Jewish Scriptures, or simply all their writings.

In fact, the understanding of the Old Testament Scriptures as prophecy represents in the best way this Christian position: all Jewish Scriptures are accepted, yet only with reference to what is new, the *euaggelion*. This latter is, of course, at first (for at least a whole generation) chiefly an oral message. However, soon, under the pressures of history, it is eventually caught up in a development so that it becomes entrusted to written form by Christian writers. This process creates the New Testament.

C. *The Formation of the New Testament Writings*

The spread of Christianity was achieved by preachers, not writers. For almost a generation the memories of Christ's life and teaching were kept by oral tradition.[23] However, we find evidence for some literary activity at the very beginnings of the Christian faith. In the opinion of many scholars, it appears very probable that the first Christian missionaries carried with them as memory aids lists of excerpts from the Old Testament as proof texts for the messiahship of Jesus as well as primitive collections of the sayings of Jesus.[24] Other literature came about by practical necessity. Paul might have been the first Christian missionary who systematically extended and multiplied his presence by sending letters to the Church communities under his care. In any case, his letters are presumably the oldest Christian literary products that have survived. In none of these literary activities, however, can we discover the intention of creating a new or additional set of "holy writings" to be used instead of or in association with the Old Testament.[25] There is, in fact, no clear evidence of the existence of a complete presentation of the life and teaching of Jesus—of a "Gospel" in the modern sense of the word—before 60 A.D. (according to many scholars not before 70 A.D.).[26] As far as our evidence goes, writing in the first decades of Christianity was secondary and subordinate to preaching and oral teaching.

We must note, however, two factors at a very early stage which, in the due course of the events, ultimately led to the development of authoritative Christian writings later assembled in the canon of the New Testament. First of all, the oral preaching about Christ is done with the claim of authority similar to that of the Old Testament. Our oldest witness for this is probably the Epistle to the Romans in which Paul presents the good news of Christ with a reference to two sets of divinely established witnesses: first "the prophets" (he is certainly referring to all the writings of the Old Testament), then the apostle himself, "set apart" by election just like the prophets for the sake of witnessing to Christ: "Paul, a servant of Christ Jesus, called to be an apostle and *set apart* to proclaim the Gospel of God, foreannounced long ago through his prophets in the Holy Scriptures" (Rom 1:1–2). The theological concepts of this text match very closely those of 1 Peter 1:10–12. According to this latter passage also the content of the Old Testament prophecies and the proclamation of "those who preach the Gospel to you" coincide. But not only the same Christ was proposed by both the prophets and the preachers of the Gospel. It is also the same Spirit of Christ who first inspired the prophets and is now at work "in power" in the ministry of the preachers of the Gospel:

They prophesied the grace that was destined to be yours. They investigated the times and circumstances which the Spirit of Christ within them was pointing to. They knew by revelation that they were providing not for themselves but for you what has now been proclaimed to you by those who preach the Gospel to you in the power of the Holy Spirit sent from heaven.

There is, indeed, sufficient evidence in the earliest documents of Christianity supporting the thesis that already the first Christian generation saw the role of the "prophets," usually accredited with the authorship of the Old Testament writings, and that of the "apostles" in manifold parallelism. The oldest such text is possibly 1 Thessalonians 2:13–15. The martyrdom of the prophets and of Jesus is set parallel to the persecution of the "apostles of Christ" (in the context: Paul, Silvanus and Timothy). The connection between "prophets and apostles" in Luke 11:49 is based on the same idea: they suffer the same destiny.[27] Yet this quotation makes more explicit than 1 Thessalonians that both groups are sent by the same one God within the framework of a common salvation history leading to the coming of Jesus who also undergoes the same destiny. We have argued elsewhere that the expression "prophets and apostles" in Luke's text does not necessarily represent a secondary rendering of the text found in Matthew (Mt 23:37) but may be a transformation of Jeremiah's formula about God's repeated and continuous sending of envoys and prophets to his people (cf. Jer 7:25 and 25:4).[28]

A second factor commonly observed by students of the Synoptic tradition is the very early tendency to stabilize the first Christian preaching into fixed formulas and accounts. The intricate data of the Synoptic problem—regardless of its solution—leave no doubt that, before the oral tradition found its way into the three compositions of Matthew, Mark and Luke, both the accounts of the events and the sayings of the Lord were solidified in smaller units faithfully repeated by carriers of an oral tradition. These two factors, the authoritative nature of the "apostolic preaching" and its tendency to reach solid and permanently fixed formulation, gave rise in due time to a literature that eventually obtained the status of "Holy Scripture" in the Christian Church alongside the writings of "Moses and the prophets."

Our Gospels themselves bear the marks of the oral tradition from which they came. The title of Mark's Gospel, for example, clearly documents the awareness of its author that his work gives written form to an orally preached message. At the time of Mark's composition, *euaggelion* is certainly a specifically Christian word meaning the content of the faith message of Christ; its use by Paul as well as by Mark himself is always connected with a proclamation *viva voce*. Now, in Mark 1:1 this became part of the introductory phase or possibly of the title of the whole composition. Should "the beginning of the good news" refer only to the passage that follows and not be the title of the whole work, there can be still little doubt about the author's intention to present in written form what, under the name of *euaggelion,* was the content of oral preaching. A similar implicit awareness of such a transition from oral to written message appears in the ending of Matthew. The passage has the role of concluding the whole work as a literary composition and therefore exposes the author's thinking about his work. In Matthew 28:16–19, Jesus gives his last precept to the disciples by committing to oral teaching—to an activity that should reach all people and must endure till the end of times—all that he has taught them. But in this we see that the book in fact ends with the command that *all of its content* be transmitted to all people of all times *by means of oral delivery.* Obviously, the author's understanding is that his book is written with the purpose of committing to writing a message originally destined to be spread by word of mouth. He is most probably aware that by choosing a new medium he helps this message to reach its intended recipients: all people in all ages. The written Gospel presents itself as the solidification, extension and prolongation of an oral message.

Also Luke's Gospel not only exhibits in its text the factual connections between oral preaching and the written book, but it also contains in its preface precious reflections about their relationship. We can summarize these reflections in the following four points:

(a) Luke's composition is one of several similar works, all trying to give an account of the events connected with Jesus.

(b) These accounts are based on information coming from first-hand witnesses who are at the same time "ministers of the word," that is, the original preachers of the good news.

(c) The composition of an orderly and reliable account appears to Luke to be an arduous task that demands continued effort and care.

(d) By undertaking this task he intends to render important service to the Christian community. The work attains apologetic value by creating recorded proof for the reliability of what the communities received orally (and, perhaps occasionally, in writing) in the form of several disconnected presentations from the traveling Christian missionaries.

These reflections of Luke reveal that the composition of his Gospel takes place in what we call today "an historical perspective." For him, the facts are somewhat remote in time, and the memories of oral tradition do not satisfy the needs of the Church anymore; they lack uniformity, coherence and order and thus jeopardize full credibility. Luke's preface contains a reflection on the composition of the Gospels as a response to the demand of the Church's life situation.

We can well understand these perceptions of Luke if we regard the upheavals of the Christian communities in the last three decades of the first century. The Jewish war ending with the destruction of Jerusalem in 70 A.D. led to the dissolution of Palestinian Christianity. This fact, combined with the disappearance of the first Christian generation by natural death, endangered the continuity of oral tradition by reducing and upsetting its social basis. The urgency of producing more permanent vehicles of transmission for the Christian message appears in this context fully understandable.

The Johannine writings, besides documenting most of our observations made above, contain frequent references to writing as an important tool for eliciting and strengthening the response of faith. The first conclusion of John's Gospel is unparalleled in the whole of the New Testament insofar as it explicitly states both the value and the limitation of written documents in serving the faith of the Church. On the one hand, the written record is only partial: "Many other signs did Jesus perform in front of his disciples which are not written in this book." On the other hand, this written record has the power and purpose to elicit faith: "These were written so that you might believe that Jesus is the Christ, the Son of God, and believing you might have life in his name" (Jn 20:30–31).[29] The close connections between the Gospel of John and the First Epistle of John entitle us to see behind the sixfold repetition "I write to you" in 1 John 2:12–14 a similar theological position. Indeed the author refers to his literary activity as other New Testament texts have referred to preaching and oral teaching. Also the Book of Revelation expresses repeated concern for writing as a means of ministry: the prophecy must be written down for the sake of the Church communities; it is the written document, protected against changes by means of blessings and curses, that is expected to be the faithful carrier of the prophet's message (cf. Rev 22:18–19).

The latest writings of the New Testament are pseudepigraphs: letters composed by anonymous authors in the name of the great personalities of the first Christian generation: Peter (I refer to 2 Peter), Paul, James and Jude.[30] The latest of them are contemporary with an ever increasing apocryphal literature that by the fourth and fifth centuries exploits every known name and personality of the New Testament by attaching them to documents that serve for edification, theology, heterodoxy, orthodoxy or just pious fantasy. The pseudepigraphs of the New Testament do not belong to this uncontrolled wild growth of "authentic documents." For many of them, centuries of critical research about their authenticity have been unable to produce a final verdict to which all scholars could adhere without reservation. But on the other end of the spectrum, certainly in 2 Peter and most probably in the pastorals, we have clear cases of pseudepigraphy done with the intention of using the names of the great apostles to spread, document and solidify their teaching as understood by the anonymous writers.

It is not our purpose to enter into the intricacies of these questions of authenticity. Nevertheless, from the very fact that these questions of authenticity pose themselves, we can draw a few useful conclusions. That by the end of the first and the beginning of the second century pseudepigraphic writings of "Paul," "Peter" or other apostolic figures come about and are eventually accepted by the Church as normative writings implies with certainty at least the following:

(a) Both the authors and the readers of these documents shared the conviction that writings from personalities like Peter and Paul should be read as authoritative texts which validly decide a question in the Church because of the authority of their authors.

(b) Reliance on the written documents coming from the first Christian generation was an experience of the Church preceding the composition of the pseudepigraphs.

(c) The Church experienced at the same time the insufficiency of the documents inherited from the past and was making efforts—through the literary activities of the anonymous authors—to include more of the content of early tradition into "authenticated" documents.

(d) The pseudepigraphs manifest also the assumption on the part of their anonymous writers that the Church widely considers the teaching of Peter, Paul and others (James, John and Jude, most probably), all considered as apostles, as normative for Christian faith.

These conclusions agree with the implications of John's first ending (Jn 20:30–31). At the turn of the first century, written documents as basis and support of faith gain increasing importance. The Church realizes the need of having in written form the "original teaching" of the first Christian apostles. However, another realization surfaces almost simultaneously: even if authenticated, written documents are not capable of answering all questions or of giving sufficient information about every desired detail or every controversial question. This wisdom is reflected in the second conclusion of John's Gospel, a conclusion to some sort of a pseudepigraphic effort to attach new material to the Gospel: "But there are also many other things which Jesus did; were every one of them to be written, I suppose that the world itself could not contain the books that would be written" (Jn 21:25). The author of this passage might have considered this unlimited increase of written documents "about the things which Jesus did" as a desirable process. He also clearly shows an awareness that having all valid apostolic teaching in written form is a practical impossibility. Thus, in some oblique way, this passage indicates, probably for the first time, that the Church must choose between a constant growth of normative writings ("things that Jesus did" would certainly be normative) or close the canon. This first realization of the need for a closed canon takes place at the time the last books of what we call today the New Testament were finished.

Positing exact dates for "the conclusion of the New Testament writings" is of course unrealistic. The dissemination and collection of these books, their successive copying and their ever increasing use require an historical process and, given the technological level of that age, demand considerable time. But the question is not only technical. At the time the last books of the New Testament are written, the sociological and historical process that eventually produces the canon of the New Testament is far from complete. (We suppose here that the very last book was 2 Peter, written about 125 A.D.)[31] Although at this time the four Gospels are already widely known, it is still customary to refer to the sayings and doings of Jesus on the basis of oral tradition. There is still quite a bit of freedom for embellishing, widening, and amplifying the original oral tradition, as a further free growth of the apocryphal literature proves. The concrete needs of the Church (devotion, curiosity, withstanding persecution, spiritual and philosophical needs or the needs of factions engaged in controversy) still influence the shaping of the tradition. Nevertheless, by some strange dialectic these changing needs themselves put on the brakes by raising the question of true tradition in the face of the multiplicity of the claims. As the question of true Christianity poses itself with increasing vigor because of the controversies over heresy, the problem of the criterion of truth obtains crucial importance.

Basically, the formation of the New Testament and the formation of its canon are two consecutive phases of the one same historical process. First, the Church produces written documents of what it considers as basic to its faith in the sense of being constitutive because it belonged to its origins. Subsequently it must face the question about the value and validity of these documents themselves in a second phase of reflection. It must struggle to establish criteria and meanwhile apply them so that distinction can be made between authentic and false documents, true and falsified traditions. As our study of the second century shows, this struggle takes place in the framework of an escalating anti-Gnostic controversy. While a complex wave of heretical movements sweep over the second century, Church leaders increasingly "cling to the apostles,"[32] and they elaborate a theological concept of apostolicity as a formula for authentic Christianity. Irenaeus' synthesis which concludes the most important formative period of the New Testament canon puts the criterion of apostolicity into the center of his system as do the other great anti-Gnostic leaders: Tertullian, Clement of Alexandria and Hippolytus of Rome.

D. *Christian Beginnings of a Theology of Inspiration*

Before we focus our attention on the process of the canonization of the books held as apostolic in the first decades of the second century, we must briefly survey the concepts that Christianity held about the Jewish Scriptures when considering them of divine authority, containing the word of God and being normative for faith and morals. This means that we should look at the beginnings of the Christian theology of inspiration in the earliest documents, basically the books which later themselves become categorized as "Sacred Scriptures." This study has its methodological importance. It will show that the parallelism between "prophets" and "apostles" has the potential to be carried further so that the latter group might be accredited also with the authorship of sacred books. Not only does the Church need criteria of faith other than the books of the Old Testament—not only is there room for new Scriptures—but there is also an obvious way of transferring the theological concepts surrounding "inspired authors" and their literary products to a new set of persons and books *provided they hold comparable roles in the history of salvation.*

It is, of course, natural that the Christian Church take over not only the sacred books of Judaism but along with them a number of concepts, terms and expressions. These appear in the first Christian documents without reservation or inhibition: "it is written," "according to the Scriptures," "Scripture says," etc. By using such introductory formulas, the writer not only means that a quotation actually comes from the holy books but that it also has decisive power and authority, that is, when it is quoted it demands a response of faith due to the word of God. There can be no doubt that the primitive Christian Church accepted the authority of the sacred books of the Old Testament without hesitation or reservation. Scripture is God's word so that "it cannot lose its force" (Jn 10:35). This conviction does not refer only to the law of Moses (i.e., the Pentateuch) but also to "the prophets" who are conceived of as the spokesmen of

God (cf. Heb 1:5–7). Even historical texts are quoted as "God's word." So for example in Matthew, Genesis 2:24 is introduced by the expression "the Creator said" although in the book of Genesis itself the verse stands as the affirmation of the human author (Mt 19:4–5).

The role of the Holy Spirit in creating the scriptural text is also an idea of Jewish origin. In Acts, the praying community quotes Psalm 2 as the work of the Holy Spirit: "You have said by the Holy Spirit through the lips of our father David, your servant" (Acts 4:25). Also in Acts, when quoting Isaiah, Paul considers the Holy Spirit to be the speaker: "The Holy Spirit stated it well when he said to your fathers through the prophet Isaiah" (Acts 28:35). The Epistle to the Hebrews repeatedly quotes Scripture with the formula "The Holy Spirit says" (Heb 3:7; 10:15). According to Mark's Gospel, Jesus himself quotes Psalm 110 as composed by David through the Holy Spirit (12:36; cf. Mt 22:42).

These formulas not only convey the recognition of the scriptural texts as sacred and authoritative but they also highlight the prophetic character of the texts. In this regard they are important theological tools for introducing and emphasizing the christological exegesis of the Old Testament texts, an issue which, as we have seen, stands at the center of the first Christian proclamation.

Our concern in this chapter will be to see how the early Church uses a Jewish concept of Holy Scriptures to develop its specifically Christian (and therefore new) insights about their role in God's plan of salvation.

Two texts, both appearing in pseudepigraphs, 2 Timothy 3:16 and 2 Peter 1:21, stand out as especially important. Their impact is due to their generality: both envisage neither this nor that quotation but the entirety of Scriptures as such.

In 2 Timothy 3:16, Paul is pictured as exhorting his choice disciple Timothy to remain faithful to the true doctrine by following the Scripture which he had known since early childhood. Here again we encounter the standard view of first century Christianity according to which the knowledge and right interpretation of the Old Testament Scriptures is a secure path leading to faith in Christ and the correct understanding of that faith. It is in this context that we should read verse 16: "All Scripture is inspired by God and is useful for teaching" (an alternative translation would be: "All divinely inspired Scripture is useful for teaching"). The Greek word *theopneus-tos* is of passive meaning with God as the cause of the action. It refers to God's "breathing," spirit-giving, inspiring activity.[33] Scripture is issued from this divine action and thus is eminently capable of teaching and strengthening the Christian community.

We must observe in passing that this text does not make reference to the human author of Scripture; instead, it regards the *text* as the product of divine inspiration. This is the first Christian text in which the concept later classified as *inspiratio objectiva* appears: the concept of the *inspired text.*

Our second passage, 2 Peter 1:21, stands in a context dealing with the problem of interpreting prophecy: "No scriptural prophecy is matter of personal interpretation. Prophecy has never been put forward by man's willing it, but men impelled by the Holy Spirit have spoken under God's influence" (2 Pet 1:20–21). The exact translation of the first words is uncertain. *Prophēteia graphēs* might mean that part of the Scriptures which can be considered in a specific sense "prophecy" (according to Jewish and also early Christian usage we can speak about law and prophets as the two parts of Scripture) or it might refer to all Scriptures insofar as they are all of prophetic nature. We have seen that in many places the New Testament regards Moses as a prophet and the Pentateuch as a group of writings with a christological meaning. It seems that 2 Peter speaks about the Holy Scriptures in general and therefore the latter interpretation is more probable. However, the text does not deal so much with the writings as with the authors of the sacred writings. These "have spoken" under the compelling influence (*pheromenoi*) of the Holy Spirit.

It is, indeed, remarkable that our text explains the origin of prophetic texts by reference to *speaking* persons, holy men *preaching* the word of God, without any apparent concern about the process of recording the speeches. This way of considering the Scriptures is based on ancient Jewish tradition. Long before the first Christian century, the Pentateuch was considered the reflection of Moses' oral preaching and teaching; as well, all psalms were globally attributed to David who "spoke" them (cf. Mk 12:36; Acts 2:25; 2:34; 4:25; Heb 4:7 etc.). Similarly all sapiential literature was customarily attributed to Solomon. It is tempting to see in these references nothing but historical errors. But it might be more insightful and profitable to regard them as expressions of a theological scheme of revelation according to which God's word reaches man through the mediating services of living persons whose election, special historical role and charismatic endowments manifest and guarantee the value and authenticity of their message. That in the history of Israel there have been such personalities with decisive and lasting influence on God's people is an unquestionable fact. But the sensitivity of the modern historian is ruffled as he sees the obvious neglect of details and precision about the ties between these particular outstanding personalities and the documents that allegedly report their activities and teaching. In spite of this neglect, however, we should not lose sight of the theological scheme conveyed through these traditional statements. They present the word of God in its interaction with human mediators fully involved in the reception and transmission of the message. They deliver God's word in the living framework of salvation history: they "speak" to us through those documents. We, the readers of the scriptural texts, are consequently taken into that same framework of history: by reading or listening to the recorded word we become disciples to the mediators of revelation. There is no question about the fact that this simple concept of the history of revelation pervades Judaism long before the beginnings of the Christian era.[34]

Our text, brief as it is, defines well the context in which Christian theology continued to consider the inspiration of biblical authors (in the language of later theologians *inspiratio subiectiva*) for many centuries. The authors of the canonical books are usually presented as charismatic leaders, prophetic persons, personalities "filled with the Holy Spirit" who deliver their message *viva voce*.[35] Being filled with the Holy Spirit assures the sacred character of what they say. Their skills in writing and the whole process of transferring the content from the medium of oral communication to writing receive little attention. Consequently, the retention or loss of historical reliability during this phase hardly ever appears as a problem of importance, while we know that modern historical criticism knows of no problem more important.

The text quoted from 2 Peter has one more feature characteristic of the approach that the primitive Church took to the question of biblical inspiration. The logical structure of the passage is namely the following: for interpreting the prophetic texts, individual human efforts are insufficient. In other words, the interpretation of inspired texts itself requires the presence of divine inspiration. Consequently one needs the testimony of the apostles, itself based on the revelation of Christ and confirmed by the word of the Father (2 Pet 1:16–19). The story of the transfiguration is quoted in order to prove that the apostles are qualified interpreters of the Old Testament. In fact, in the later usage of the Church, the word "inspiration" retains a meaning equally applicable to biblical authors and biblical exegetes. It simply refers to the action of the Holy Spirit moving mind and will to elicit insights, to motivate actions, to bring about decisions, and to prompt external activities. This concept of inspiration remains too wide to be applied specifically to biblical inspiration as such. However, it keeps the requirement of "continued inspiration" alive, demanding that the texts be interpreted "in the same spirit" in which they were written.[36]

The concepts of inspiration taken over from Judaism are easily adaptable to cover the case of the "apostolic writings." The authors of the earliest products of Christian literature might be to a large extent unknown figures. Yet, just as it was in the case of the Old Testament prophets, we can accredit their content to the preaching of those important personalities who played a decisive role in the history of revelation in its Christian phase. Their direct influence on the documents in question might remain unspecified and yet a theological scheme can be affirmed: These documents represent their "words," their "preaching," their "precepts." They are their writings in a global sense that the popular understanding might reduce to a simple scheme: they are the writings of the apostles. Furthermore, the apostles are also thought of as imbued with the Spirit, doing their missionary work with a "fullness of the Spirit," a fact that the ending of each canonical Gospel emphasizes in its own way. Paul's concept of apostolicity or the idea of 1 Peter about the "evangelizers" is not different in this respect. Even if the exact historical content of the concept "apostles" remains blurred, there are enough concrete historical personalities to refer to (Peter, Paul, John, James, if necessary "the Twelve") who specify the connection between these normative persons and the "Norm of Norms," Jesus himself. After all, "the prophets" and "the law and the prophets" are also concepts with blurred edges, and yet they function very well when used to highlight the authority of a group of sacred writings. Modern authors are quite exact as they point out that the concepts of "the apostles" is not a merely historical category but a "theologoumenon,"[37] a concept created with historical references but foremost with a theological content. However, we must realize that this "theologoumenon" was created according to the pattern of another similar concept, that of "the prophets" designating the "authors" of the Old Testament. With this background in mind, we might become more receptive to the idea of forming the canon on the basis of "apostolicity" since it follows the pattern of holding sacred other Scriptures, those that were said to be "prophetic," the outcome of the activities of "the prophets."

E. *The Development of the Canonical Principle in the Second Century*
    For the development of the New Testament canon, the most crucial period is the first half of the second century. Study of this period is made difficult because of the scarcity of the documents and the uncertainties about their provenance and dating. So, for example, the *Didache* and the *Letter of Barnabas* are extremely difficult to date without allowing a margin of forty to fifty years. The same is true about the earliest portion of the available Gnostic literature. Many of our difficulties are rooted in the rapid cultural change in the Church's ethnic background, the transition from Jewish to Hellenistic thought patterns. We know little about the details of this transformation. We only know that the two Jewish wars accelerated it violently. The often mentioned allegation that the development of the canon was promoted largely under the pressures of the Gnostic movement is, in general, plausible. But when we try to ascertain the details we are constantly handicapped by uncertainties concerning the chronological sequence of the known texts. The most important Gnostic leaders, Valentinus and Marcion, are only indirectly known through the writings of their disciples and their opponents. Given this state of affairs, the question of methodology is extremely important. Since several conclusions might depend on the premises taken for granted, we must not prejudice the outcome of our research with uncritically assumed presuppositions. Therefore, we shall try to fol-

low a narrow path, roughly paved and poorly lit, yet sufficiently marked by a small number of ascertainable facts and based on documents with sufficiently established provenance and dating. We should avoid the use of hypotheses as much as possible and hope that from the texts pertaining to the first half of the century we can decipher the coherent outline of a development that connects the formative period of the New Testament and the initial reflections on the canon leading to the synthesis of Irenaeus.

1. Clement of Rome

The first letter of Clement, dated with virtual unanimity at 96 or 97 A.D., contains important passages on "apostolicity" as a theological concept formed about the role and function of the first preachers of the Christian faith. As it appears in 1 Clement, this concept is deeply rooted in the Synoptic tradition and Paul's self-understanding manifested in his letters. It contains, however, some special features characteristic for Clement's time and the subsequent decades, usually referred to as the "subapostolic" age. Clement's main ideas about "the apostles" can be summarized as follows:

(a) The model of Christian revelation consists of a chain of agents of transmission, linked together: God—Jesus Christ—apostles—appointed bishops and deacons.[38]

(b) The "Gospel" is the content of this revelation; the linkage of the transmitting agents assures the arrival of the authentic message to the contemporary faithful.[39]

(c) The "apostles" are usually referred to as an anonymously collective group; only Peter and Paul are mentioned by name.[40]

(d) The "apostles" are presented as similar to Moses and the prophets in two respects. On the one hand, they all possessed God-given authority and inspiration;[41] on the other hand, all of them became victims of jealousy, rejection and hatred leading to martyrdom.[42]

(e) The Church is in possession of the apostolic testimony mostly by remembering it, i.e., by the surviving oral tradition which itself is based on the continued existence of the Church in its structured form, with bishops and deacons. The written documents issued by the apostles are also mentioned.[43] Clement considers Paul "truly inspired" when writing his First Letter to the Corinthians (1 Cor is quoted), but the existence of written sources for Paul's teaching constitutes only a small part of the total picture. Clement obviously considers the succession of bishops and deacons into the roles and functions of the apostles more important. He also seems to refer to the extant memory of the apostles' teachings and admonitions and the lasting value of their testimony through martyrdom without reference to written sources.

(f) "Scripture" means the writings of the Old Testament. Yet in two different ways there appears sufficient evidence that for Clement the memories of the apostolic teaching (oral or written) and the Holy Scriptures taken over from Judaism are to be juxtaposed as of comparable value. On the one hand, the quotations from the Old Testament are used in repeated parallelism with the sayings of the Lord[44] or the teaching based on apostolic authority.[45] On the other hand, with a variety of techniques, the scriptural quotations are made suitable to become Christian teaching. They are either treated as prophecy fulfilled in the deeds and words of Christ, or they are quoted as moral guidelines given by Christ and the Holy Spirit[46] in times preceding the coming of the Messiah. Quite often the Old Testament is simply quoted as material containing divinely established moral norms that must be applied to Christians without, however, supposing or imposing Jewish customs, ritual laws or identification with Judaism as an ethnic group.[47]

Undeniably, 1 Clement is deeply embedded in the Old Testament and succeeds in using the Scriptures abundantly without either a return to Judaism or the reliance on the dangerous tool of allegory. The repeated assertion of the importance of studying the Scriptures shows that scriptural quotations are not merely of illustrative nature. The author draws his material from a conscious study of the Scriptures conducted under Christian guidelines: the light of faith in Christ as Messiah and Savior. It has been argued that Clement's Old Testament quotations are taken from some prepared "florilegium" of passages.[48] If so, we can see in First Clement the outcome of a conscious effort to exploit the Old Testament for Christian teaching by the method of *selective* use. Guidelines *for what to select* come from "the Lord's words" and "the teaching of the apostles." *In such exegetical practice the principles of a Christian canon of Holy Scriptures already make their first appearance with more or less explicitness.* We can formulate these principles in two statements:

(a) The teachings of the Lord and of the apostles, recalled from memory or quoted from documents, are intermingled and juxtaposed with the *graphē* of old since they share the same authority of divine origin.

(b) The new teaching is less precisely defined because it is mostly quoted from oral tradition. However, it obtains "the upper hand" by guiding the use and interpretation of the Jewish writings.

2. IGNATIUS OF ANTIOCH

The letters of Ignatius show that many of the ideas found in the letter of Clement to the Corinthians are familiar to the members of other Churches. Ignatius, for example, has the same "anonymous" concept of apostolicity. Although he speaks of apostles at least fifteen times, he mentions by name only Peter and Paul. These he names twice when referring to the original messengers of the faith in a particular Church (Rome and Ephesus). In this context he also mentions Paul's Letter to the Ephesians.[49] Most revealing is his comparison of the apostles to the presbyters:[50] he considers the apostles as a collegial group[51] united around Christ by a common faith and function. The relationship of this "apostolic college" to the twelve apostles of the Synoptic Gospels is not entirely clear. Yet in one text Ignatius strongly underlines the testimonial value of "those with Peter" who have seen Jesus after his resurrection, touched him, ate and drank with him.[52] He repeatedly mentions that the apostolic group is gathered around Jesus as the presbyters gathered around the bishop.[53] Of course, this model recalls the general conception of the Twelve as it is presented in the Synoptics: chosen disciples surrounding Jesus in his public ministry. One is therefore inclined to think that for Ignatius "the apostles" means first and most of all "the Twelve." However, by calling Paul an apostle he blurs the identification, a fact that remains constant in both the theological reflection and the popular piety of the Church throughout the centuries. There is nothing surprising in this fact if you realize the "elasticity" of the concept in the various documents of the New Testament. Since the concept of apostleship allows a wider and a narrower acceptance, it remains at times vague and unclear who exactly are meant to be included in the group.

Most important is Ignatius' concept of normativity. He considers normative not only the teaching of Jesus or "the Gospel"[54] but also the preaching of the prophets[55] and the precepts of the apostles.[56] The ultimate norm is Christ, identified with "the Gospel." He is anticipated or fore-announced by the prophets and then extended through the apostles. Here, in fact, we can detect the forerunner of the Christian canon of Scripture as norm of faith: "prophets" (Old Testament)—Christ (the Gospel or Gospels)—"the apostles" (different writings, mostly in the form of letters, attributed to different apostles).[57]

And yet, Ignatius has hardly any place for *Scriptures* as such when presenting his vision of the order of salvation. In his texts, the prophets and the apostles mostly appear as preachers, not authors of books or authorities behind certain important written documents. This tendency of personalizing revelation is most obvious when he identifies the Gospel "with the coming of the Savior, our Lord Jesus Christ, his passion and resurrection"[58] or simply with "Jesus in the flesh."[59] In Ignatius' conception the patriarchs, the prophets and the apostles appear as contemporaneous and coexistent with the Church as a living community which he calls "the unity of God." Thus apostolic *succession* as such cannot be spoken of because the linear pattern of history almost disappears in this great panoramic vision of salvation history. The connective links of revelation "God—Jesus—apostles" are mirrored in the corresponding structures of the Church consisting of "bishop—deacon—presbyters." These earthly structures express, symbolize, represent (and make present) the heavenly reality. Jesus with his prophets and apostles continues his presence in the Church in a quasi-sacramental, mystical way. It is faith that enables us to attain the spiritual realities through the visible, "fleshly" structures.

One might ask if Ignatius' presentation of the protagonists of salvation history as contemporaries in the framework of a liturgical assembly did not entirely do away with the historical dimension of revelation. This is definitely not the case. His insistence on the priority of the Gospel (= Christ) makes him also assert that the prophets anticipated him and that the apostles transmitted him to later ages.

In other words, the dependence of the prophets and the apostles on Jesus necessarily appears in a temporal pattern. It is the Church that is made atemporal by Ignatius, not the process of salvation history. As we read Irenaeus or Tertullian or Clement of Alexandria we detect in retrospect that Ignatius' loyalty to both the Old Testament and the truth of the incarnation, in fact, prepares their ammunition for the Church's anti-Gnostic battle which is to reach its first peak within a few decades after his death.

3. DIDACHE

At first sight it is the title of the *Didache* that appears to be most significant for our topic: "The Teaching of the Twelve Apostles." It reveals both that doctrine of apostolic origin is normative for the Church and that apostolic authority ultimately resides with the Twelve who accompanied Christ in his earthly life. But there are also further passages in the document which reveal other aspects of the concept of apostolicity although they do not coalesce into a unified doctrine or vision. In fact, the historical perspective is quite absent from the *Didache:* it does not exhibit the consciousness of the Church becoming increasingly distant from its own origins or being under constraint to look at its own past and heritage.

In the first part of the work, dealing with "The Two Ways," we find "the Way of Life" described with the abundant use of scriptural material. Its arrangement is peculiar. At first we find a positive presentation of Christian morality that uses extensively the Matthean/ Lukan tradition of the Sermon on the Mount. In this part no Old Testament text is quoted.[60] From the beginning of Chapter 2, however, a series of negative commands is listed, starting with elements of the Ten Commandments and continuing with further quotations, all taken from the Old Testament. In other words, we are dealing with a composition that sets moral guidelines from both specifically Christian and Jewish (Old Testament) sources and juxtaposes the two kinds of materials without mixing them. The author definitely shows awareness that these two blocks of moral precepts are of a twofold origin. To what extent he is conscious that to these two different sources he attributes equal divine authority is hard to tell. One might even speculate that the New Testament texts (quoted from oral tradition or by free adjustment of the written Synoptic sources)[61] obtain *de facto* priority over the Old Testament quotations since they set the tone of the section by prescribing the general rules of attitude and behavior while the Old Testament texts are only applied to prohibit specific misdeeds.

The concept of apostleship is seriously blurred in the *Didache* by the fact that it is intermingled with references to prophets and prophecy. Robert Kraft is right in stating that in this work "the 'apostles' seem to be roughly synonymous with the 'prophets.' "[62] Most telling in this regard is the remark that if an "apostle" does not behave according to certain set rules, he should be considered a "false prophet." We easily recognize here the same blending of the ministries of "apostles" and "prophets" that appears in Ephesians[63] and stands in contrast with the careful distinction emphasized by Paul in 1 Corinthians.[64] The statement of Chapter 15 according to which "bishops and deacons" perform the tasks of prophets and teachers obscures the issue even further and indicates that in this work the concept of New Testament prophecy is applicable to any kind of spiritual leadership role. Nevertheless, the author is quite conscious of the distinction between Church prophets and "the prophets of old." The latter he considers models for shaping the behavior of the Christian prophets.

In general we may say that one of the most important preoccupations that appears in the *Didache* is that of distinguishing false prophets from the true ones. The need of practical discriminatory norms for telling apart true and false prophecy is closely comparable with the later problem of the canon. The only difference appears to be that the *Didache* is concerned with oral and not written sources of doctrine. How does the author of the *Didache* attempt to solve the problem about true and false prophecy? His answers come mostly from the Synoptic (oral) tradition which he applies and extrapolates in order to give detailed precepts about the reception of the traveling teachers. But also he produces this book of his as an instrument to be used by the Churches, and he gives his presentation under the title of "The Doctrine of the Twelve Apostles." *We see here the principle of apostolicity at work: it leads to the production of literary works enshrining old oral tradition and is used to give maximum authority to the resulting written work.*

While the practical criteria of the *Didache* are obviously insufficient for distinguishing true and false "prophecy" (teaching), their
becoming part of a written document testifies that the author sees no
better way of settling such questions than by means of written documents of apostolic origin. In this respect, the *Didache* is a typically
"second century work," signaling the movement from oral tradition
to written documents and advancing the principle of apostolicity as a
tool of settling doctrinal questions.[65]

4. THE LETTER OF BARNABAS

This document is particularly difficult to date. The limits of dating are widely set between 70 A.D. and 135 A.D. There is, however,
considerable evidence that the work belongs in its present form to
the first decades of the second century rather than to the last decades
of the first.[66] In the way that the figures of the apostles are presented
we see the signs of considerable distance in time. The apostles are
said to be "those destined to preach his (Christ's) Gospel," chosen
"from among the worst type of sinners" so that it would become evident that Christ's mission was to the sinners, not to the saints.[67] They
were the Twelve; their number corresponds to the twelve tribes of Israel. But they are also conveniently symbolized by the three children
sprinkling the blood of the sacrificial heifer on the people (cf. Num
19:1–10).[68] These remarks presuppose the basic data of the Synoptic
Gospels but they also exhibit a good amount of theological reflection
and the use of symbolism, something that supposes the elapse of several decades after the death of the first Christian generation. The
"twelve apostles" as referred to by the Barnabas letter do not seem to
be people of recent memory. We look in vain for any imprint of indi-
viduality: Barnabas mentions no apostle by name. This fact, of
course, further completes a development already discernible in Clement of Rome and Ignatius.[69]

The main concern of the letter is to teach about the Christian
use of the Old Testament. The basic concept of the exegesis it offers
corresponds to the oldest tradition of the Church. What Paul wrote
in Romans 15:4 ("Everything written before our time was written for
our instruction") Barnabas considers as a program to be carried out
in detail by showing that, indeed, all parts of the Old Testament can

be claimed legitimately as Christian Scriptures. He makes further inroads into the mass of Jewish inheritance[70] by the use of diverse techniques. What he intends to obtain is "gnosis,"[71] the appropriation of the deeply hidden ultimate meaning of the texts. This is possible only in virtue of Christian revelation and the actual influence of the Holy Spirit, also coming from Christ.[72] Thus, for him, the Jewish understanding of the Scriptures is not only insufficient, it is, by the nature of what the Old Testament is, impossible. He legitimates the finding of christological meaning in the texts by attributing their origin to the pre-existing Son speaking through the prophets before the time of his arrival in the flesh.[73] Equivalently, he would refer to the anticipated knowledge of Jesus by the prophets through the Spirit.[74] These principles are not *per se* new. New, however, is the boldness with which the author divests the old texts of their original meaning and turns them, by the use of diverse exegetical approaches, into texts with specifically Christian meaning.

For our topic, what is most important is the delicate situation that the Old Testament obviously occupies in the communities for which Barnabas writes. The author makes every attempt to disentangle his Christian faith from its Jewish cradle yet without losing the possession of any part of the Old Testament Scriptures. By a systematic "Christianization" of these writings he wants to achieve two aims. He exploits them fully for Christian teaching but at the same time he reduces as much as possible any resemblance of historical continuity between the Church and the Jewish past they represent. Thus, the use of allegory in the sense of typology or of other modes of symbolism is aimed in Barnabas at diluting the Old Testament into cryptic passages that were undecipherable or misleading for the historical environment for which they had been written.[75]

The lack of care for historical continuity with Jewish roots is not a result of well-meaning awkwardness when using the dangerous tools of allegory. Rather, it manifests an almost schizophrenic mentality with regard to Christianity's Jewish origins. On the one hand, we see an effort to assimilate all Scriptures into specifically Christian use; on the other hand, this effort is carried out with a motivation to minimize continuity with the Jewish past.

The letter of Barnabas offers the best insights for understanding the plight of the Church from which the Gnostic crisis and especially the heresy of Marcion sprang up. The letter expresses most eloquently the ambition of developing a Christian "gnosis" as a sophisticated and culturally "up-to-date" presentation of the Christian teaching. In this endeavor, the author found himself confronted with a dilemma. The traditional terms of his faith obliged him to deepen his understanding of the Christian message by searching the Scriptures. At the same time, the growing Gentile element in the Church became increasingly intolerant of the Jewish past of their religion, to which they felt no ties of national or historical belonging and against which they had shared the animosity of a great segment of their society, a result of the two Jewish wars. For understanding the "Christian dilemma" of the first fifty years of the second century we must always keep in mind the massive forces embedded in the Gospel tradition and in Paul's heritage, forces which demand organic ties with the Jewish past. Yet there were the equally strong cultural and political tendencies calling the Church to radicalize the formal break with Judaism which had already become an irrevocable reality at the end of the first century. This is the context in which Marcion finds fuel for burning the last bridge, namely the books of the Old Testament, and in which the anti-Gnostic Church Fathers justify the keeping of the Jewish heritage with a christological exegesis, developed with Hellenistic tools and permeated with a universalistic vision of salvation history.

5. EARLY GNOSTIC SOURCES

The fragmentary and rather diverse Gnostic material pertaining to the second century constitutes a meager but important source for the history of the canon. Unfortunately, the texts are not only scarce but also often elusive and difficult to interpret. Consequently we cannot attempt any systematization. However, we can state two basic facts supported by the convergent testimony of the disperse data.

(a) *The principle of apostolicity* is not only uncontested throughout but occasionally directly affirmed. Most obvious proof for that is the attribution of many Gnostic Gospels to one of the twelve apostles.[76]

Apostolicity as a criterion of revealed truth appears in the use of the quotation formula "the apostle says" or "said." We find it in writings as early and disparate as the *Letter to Flora* by Ptolemy (quoting Jn 1:3 and 1:11),[77] in the Gnostic *Treatise on Resurrection* (for Rom 8:17 and Eph 2:5–6)[78] and frequently in the fragments of Theodotos preserved by Clement of Alexandria. In this latter document *ho apostolos* means most often Paul,[79] the most often quoted apostolic author, but it also introduces quotations from John[80] and 1 Peter.[81] Once even Luke's Gospel is quoted with this formula: "As the apostle said, peace on earth and glory in the highest" (cf. Lk 2:14).[82] All these texts come from the middle of the second century, with the latest time limit being around 160–170 A.D. Since they belong to the Valentinian gnosis, one might plausibly conclude that the quotation formula was first introduced by the Valentinians as a means of using various texts of apostolic claim for supporting their own speculations.[83] Certainly the Valentinians showed no preference for one apostle to the exclusion of the others. Consequently, in the quotation formula, *ho apostolos* is not to be interpreted in an exclusive sense. In such a context "the apostle says" resembles the well-known formula "the prophet says" by which any sort of prophetic text can be quoted. It does not designate one apostle as *the* apostle *par excellence,*[84] but simply emphasizes the apostolic authority of the author to whom the text is attributed. That it is used with growing preference instead of the names of the various apostles is well in accordance with the anonymity of the apostles as they are referred to routinely throughout the second century.[85]

(b) In general, most of the Gnostic texts show broad-minded freedom in the way they handle traditional material. The principle of apostolicity does not appear as a limiting factor but rather as a tool by which a diversity of sources can be assembled. By asserting their belief in the actual presence of the Spirit or of the Logos, the Gnostics easily give account of their position that upholds the existence of continued revelation. Interesting in this regard is Christ's exchange with his disciples as reported by the *Gospel of Thomas:*

> His disciples said to him: Twenty-four prophets spoke in Israel and all of them spoke in you.

The claim is known: all prophecies of old were uttered by virtue of

the presence of Christ, the eternal Son or Logos.[86] But Jesus' answer
is surprising:

> You have omitted the one living in your presence and have
> spoken of the dead.[87]

This response seems to relegate Old Testament prophecy to the
realm of the obsolete and states the absolute superiority of Christ
whose living presence makes the old prophecies superfluous.

Of course, Gnostic speculations go beyond the prophetic and
apostolic sources and they do not present any justification for doing
so. It seems, however, that the frequent Gnostic claim of presenting
secret apostolic tradition was mostly motivated by the aim of harmo-
nizing the principle of apostolicity with their freedom for cosmological, psychological and metaphysical speculation. Claiming such
traditions obviously precludes any objection based on the observation that the Gnostic teacher's position is not supported by any
known traditional source. He can always reply that the apparent lack
of traditional support is the necessary result of secrecy. It seems that
the widespread custom of claiming to draw from secret apostolic tradition is a strong argument proving that the use of the principle of
apostolicity was equally common. Thus, while claiming the possession of secretly transmitted apostolic traditions, the Gnostics tried to
evade the controlling force of Church tradition; by doing so they did
in fact give witness to the principle of apostolicity as the common
ground which they shared with their opponents.

6. MARCION

As we have noted above, most of the Gnostic material from the
second century which we found relevant to our topic is of Valentinian origin.[88] In Valentinianism there is no sign of effort to establish a
closed canon. Rather there are indications to the contrary: nothing is
particularly rejected or excluded. Theodotos is ready to refer to any
apostolic authority if such a text appears to be useful for the gnosis
he is seeking. Such an eclectic attitude may not be exclusively characteristic of the Valentinians. By the middle of the second century
the conflation of various Gospel traditions appears to be common

practice. *Papyrus Egerton 2* coming from around the middle of the century shows signs of "contact" with all four canonical Gospels.[89] According to Origen, Basilides composed a Gospel harmony.[90] And, of course, the Valentinian *Gospel of Truth* reflects both Synoptic and Johannine material.[91]

What we know about Marcion stands in sharp contrast with the eclectic openness of the Valentinians. His thought is marked by exclusiveness, limitation and systematization with regard to the written sources circulating in the Church of his time. No wonder that he has been accredited with a major role in the early development of the New Testament canon.

There is little doubt that Marcion played a major role in the development of the canon. However, to assess and evaluate his role, we are strongly handicapped by total lack of original texts by Marcion himself and, really, of any substantial information about him or his teaching from contemporary sources. Reconstructions such as that of Harnack fall into the danger of selecting, for the sake of supporting certain hypotheses, only those statements of our anti-Marcionite sources (mainly Irenaeus and Tertullian) which fit them while dismissing other texts on the basis of the anti-Marcionite bias of their authors.[92]

It is uncontested that Marcion's basic option consisted in total rejection of the Old Testament. That this decision was motivated largely by the anti-Jewish sentiments following the Bar Kochba revolt is plausibly argued for by Grant.[93] But the painstaking and, to a large extent, unconvincing efforts of the Epistle of Barnabas to find Christian meaning in every part of the Jewish Scriptures demonstrate another aspect of the problem. As Christianity penetrated deeper and deeper into the Hellenistic culture of the Roman world the Jewish heritage became a liability, a burden carried with growing difficulties. Thus Marcion had more than enough reasons to break out of the Jewish matrix and abolish the problem of Christian exegesis by one radical option. Tertullian insists that Marcion's motivation was a philosophical one: he was intrigued by the problem of evil. When establishing two ultimate principles, the "just" and vindictive Creator of the Old Testament and the good and merciful God of Jesus Christ, he solved a problem torturing many contemporary philosophers.[94] The presence of all these motives might be safely assumed in the

Marcionite phenomenon: if they all do not apply to Marcion, they seem to explain the impressive response that his movement received within a short period of time. They also explain why the Marcionite movement was capable of surviving as an institution for several centuries.

It can be easily seen that the Marcionite rejection of the Old Testament means breaking with a consistent position held by the Church since its beginnings. One must note in particular that, regardless of Marcion's option *for* Paul, his breaking ties with the Old Testament stands in contradiction to all Pauline letters and, really, the heart of Paul's teaching.

Did Marcion establish (for the first time) a collection of sacred Christian books in order to replace the *graphai* of old which he had rejected? This suggestion appears logical enough if we regard the function of written documents in the Church's daily life, especially in worship and catechesis. Given the preponderant role of the Old Testament as Scripture in both liturgy and teaching, the rejection of these writings must have created a practical vacuum to be filled by a new collection of books. Nevertheless, we must caution against any conclusions based on the assumption that the books of Marcion's canon are a reaction to the Church's alleged neglect of Paul.[95] We must examine Marcion's choice of sacred books on the basis of what we know about the use of "the prophets and the apostles" as the source of teaching at his time.

The formula of referring to "the prophets and the apostles" as the normative source of Christian teaching is firmly anchored in the pre-Marcionite Church. It surfaces regularly whenever questions are raised about doctrine. It implies, of course, the acceptance of the Old Testament as God's word and its Christian exegesis which can be traced back to the beginnings of Christianity. At the time Marcion makes his appearance, Polycarp of Smyrna[96] and the anonymous author of 2 Clement[97] use these expressions to refer to the sources of Church teaching. That "apostles" means, already before Marcion, not only an oral tradition but a tradition passed down also in the form of writing is also commonly assumed as it is attested by Ignatius, Clement of Rome and 2 Peter. They all know about the preservation of Paul's letters written to particular Churches and make reference to them. It is also commonly assumed that the Synoptic material known to these authors reached them by the double channel of oral and written tradition. In any case, Marcion did not discover Paul as a writer or as *the* apostle with a written heritage.

There seem to be three questions, however, which we should investigate more closely to see the specific role of innovation, played by Marcion. These are:

1. Is the bipartite division of the New Testament Scriptures (*euaggelion* and *apostolikon*) his invention?

2. How should we interpret his decision to have only one Gospel in relation to the *later* anti-Marcionite reaction asserting the principle of a fourfold ("tetramorphous") Gospel?

3. How is Marcion's reduction of "the apostles" to "the apostle" (Paul) to be explained in light of his contemporaries?

To the first question, H. von Campenhausen answers in the affirmative and considers the statement as the most certain fact about Marcion's creative originality promoting the New Testament canon.[98] Also according to John Knox, the grouping of the writings of the New Testament into one Gospel and "the apostle" (ten letters of Paul) was the most important single step by which Marcion determined the shape of the future canon.[99] The Catholic reaction was, he says, nothing else than the extension of "the Gospel" to a fourfold composition and the inclusion of the pastorals and other non-Pauline letters into the second part and, of course, the insertion of Acts as a bridge connecting the Gospels and the apostolic letters in the middle.[100] (The admission of the Book of Revelation is like "an appendix" to this whole story and it did not substantially influence the structure of the canon.) Thus the canon would have come about as an attempt to counterbalance Marcion's one-sided Paulinism by adding new material. But the basic structure and shape of the canon were determined by the collection of writings produced by Marcion.

This reconstruction, however attractive, does not sufficiently respect the developments preceding Marcion. First of all, already in the pre-Marcionite Church, the concepts "Gospel" and "apostle" are combined in a dialectic way. The older usage, well attested by Paul, speaks about "Gospel" (*euaggelion*) as the object of the apostolic preaching. St. Paul considers himself as "set apart for the Gospel" (Rom 1:1), that is, identifying his apostleship with the task of proclaiming the Gospel. We find this usage in other early documents as well. But also in the early sources sometimes the Lord and the apostles are presented in historical succession; then the Christian tradition receives a bipartite form: precepts of the Lord and the commands of the apostles. Since the material pertaining to the Lord is more and more frequently called "Gospel" and it often appears distinguished from the directives of the apostles, the bipartite form of "Gospel–apostles" surfaces very early. "I take refuge," Ignatius writes, "in the Gospel which to me is Jesus in the flesh and in the apostles" (Philad 5:1). He speaks to the content of his faith as "the decrees of the Lord and the apostles" (Magn 13). Also Polycarp's letter refers to the New Testament in a bipartite formula: "as he (Christ) commanded us and the apostles who preached the Gospel to us." But, of course, for him (as well as for Ignatius) for the fullness of doctrine we need also the Old Testament: "and the prophets who foretold the coming of our Lord."[101]

What seems to be a first instance in the case of Marcion is the distinction of *euaggelion* and *apostolikon* as *books* or collections of books. But this is understandable from the option that Marcion made. Should the naming of the two parts of the Marcionite Scriptures really go back to Marcion (this assumption is based on one sentence by Epiphanius)[102] its explanation must be found in the choice of Paul as the only authentic apostle. For the pre-Marcionite Church *hoi apostoloi* was an adequate term to describe *all* New Testament revelation because it obviously included the Gospel traditions. When Marcion chose Paul and excluded the other apostles (in particular "the Twelve") his *ho apostolos* became a less inclusive formula. It was not possible to refer by it to the Synoptic material since Paul was by no means a witness to the events of Jesus' life and sayings. In the Catholic tradition the main formula remains, well into the twelfth century, that of "prophets and apostles" to describe the totality of revelation. And when they speak about the New Testament as "Gospel" (or "Gospels") and "apostles" (always in the plural) this distinction is not imposed by any necessity since "the apostles" always include the witnesses of the Gospel narratives. Thus we see that Marcion's innovation is rooted in his choice of reducing "the apostles" to one single apostle, a decision on which we will have to make some further observations. He hardens the distinction "Gospel–apostle" into a clear-cut division because his Gospel is not guaranteed or supported by the one single apostle whose authority he recognizes.

Our second question refers to Marcion's adherence to only one Gospel. Irenaeus and Tertullian chastise him for rejecting Matthew, Mark and John and claim that his Gospel is that of Luke interpolated and abbreviated for the sake of theological objectives.[103] The basis of their argument is clear: for them, Matthew, Mark and John are of apostolic authority while Marcion's rejection is based on his suspicion that all the apostles besides Paul have distorted the original message of Jesus. It is worth noticing that there is no indication that Marcion had rejected the apostolic origin of those other Gospels. He rejected the other apostles themselves and thus had to settle with one Gospel which he hoped to have restored to its original purity. It is rightfully pointed out, however, that at the time of Marcion the "fourfold Gospel canon" claimed by Irenaeus was not known as yet. Our best proof is Tatian's *Diatessaron* but there might be other examples. The Gospel of Basilides was possibly a harmony of earlier Gospels. In any case, combining various Gospel accounts and traditions is not uncommon in the middle of the second century. The fate of Tatian's work in the Syrian Church shows that, at the time his Gospel was compiled, the composition of one coherent Gospel narrative to replace the variety of Gospels was an accepted operation. *For that* Tatian was not considered a heretic. Thus, according to all indications, Marcion's conflict with the Church at large is not rooted in disagreements about books but in his rejection of "the prophets" and the replacement of the apostles by one single apostle. It is again this latter option that is the basis of discord about the Gospel narratives. He rejects the other Gospels and, rather than conflating the different traditions (as Tatian and the Valentinians do), creates a "Pauline Gospel"—a Gospel that stands in agreement with his interpretation of Paul.

Our third question concerns Marcion's choice of Paul as the only apostle. Although he is definitely wrong in his understanding of Paul, it seems that, from the available choices, Paul was the only logical candidate to opt for. Besides Paul's anti-Jewish polemics, the incident reported in Galatians between Peter and Paul himself gave sufficient motivation for Marcion to exploit a documented "antithesis" that sets apostle against apostle and, from this point of departure, to employ Paul's writings in support of a dualistic understanding of salvation history. The fact that Galatians[104] stands at the head of the Marcionite canon certainly supports this interpretation. We should not forget, however, that Marcion chose Paul first of all because he had to choose an apostle. He had to present his views as all his contemporary fellow Christians did: basing his statement on what "the apostle said." The only difference was that, now in the context of Marcionism, *ho apostolos* became an exclusive formula meaning the one and only one worthy of being called an apostle of Christ.

From the above observations, it seems to follow logically: Marcion was the first Christian teacher to present a closed canon. The closure of his canon came about by excluding books other than the Marcionite Gospel and the ten Pauline epistles. And, indeed, it might be more correct to talk about exclusion rather than closure. In the case that Marcion's own *Antitheses* was granted privileged position among the Scriptures of the Marcionite Church, the Marcionite "closure" of the canon appears certainly doubtful. But even if that was not the case, the "closure" that he has established needs to be qualified. It was aimed at restricting the canon to the heritage of one apostle at the exclusion of the Twelve, rather than being the fruit of the realization that the formation period of the Church came to an end and thus the Church of the beginnings became the norm and guide for subsequent periods. When the anti-Gnostic Church settled for a closed canon because it acknowledged only apostolic books, the closure of the canon came about as a decision flowing from the principle of apostolicity against any other claim of later norms. Thus it seems that the closure of the canon as it happened after Marcion had a meaning different from what Marcion had in mind. Therefore, even for the closure of the canon, Marcion's role as that of the innovator is not to be misunderstood. Formally, he was the first to give his communities an exclusive list of recognized apostolic books but he did so by a conscious rejection of "the other apostles," an option clearly heretical according to accepted standards of the contemporary Church at large. We must grant, however, that the anti-Marcionite reactions of Irenaeus and later of Tertullian have proved that

Marcion's heresy acted as an important stimulus for the further development and finalization of the canon.

7. JUSTIN MARTYR

Justin should be treated not only as Marcion's contemporary but also as an independent witness of Christian thinking and teaching concerning the status of the canon in the middle of the second century. There is no substantial evidence that, besides occasional references condemning Marcion, his extant works had a direct anti-Marcionite purpose.

In Justin we can find the then traditional reference to the prophets and the apostles as carriers of the teachings in which Christians believe. However, when presenting this topic, Justin reveals some special features.

(a) Justin speaks of "apostles and prophets" rather than putting them in the more traditional order of "prophets and apostles." Of course his formula is also very ancient: it is found in Ephesians (2:20, 3:5 and 4:11). There, however, the expression envisages, in all probability, Church prophets and not the prophets of old, while Justin's formulas certainly speak about the prophets of the Old Testament. The order found in Justin possibly reflects these deutero-Pauline texts. Later, both Tertullian[105] and Clement of Alexandria[106] quote Ephesians in reference to New and Old Testament. More probably, however, Justin expresses a new approach to the sources of Christian teaching: that of Gentile Christianity. For him, as Knox correctly recognized, "the Jewish Bible became as truly and completely Christian as the Gospels."[107] Justin carried the Christian expropriation of the Old Testament Scriptures further than anybody before him. His Logos theory is a remarkable attempt to unify salvation history and make it appear co-extensive with the history of mankind. God with his ever-present Logos reached out to erring man at every time and place. He was present not only to the Jews through the prophets but also to the Greeks whose philosophers obtained from him their valid insights. Such a concept of revelation oversteps the boundaries of Jewish history and reaches a perspective of cultural universalism. But Justin has to go further: he has to explain how the message of the prophets finally reached its destination by revealing the meaning of Christ to the searching mind. If the original addressees of the prophecies, namely the Jews, have not accepted the faith of Christ, what purpose did the prophecies serve? Justin thinks that while the prophets were maltreated and rejected just as Christ was among the Jews, nonetheless their message was joyfully received by the Gentiles who "were filled with joy and faith, turned away from their idols and dedicated themselves to the unbegotten God through Christ" (*Dialogue with Trypho* 119.6). At this moment, as he continues in the same text, the apostles "gave over to them (the Gentiles) the prophecies." From the point of view of Gentile Christianity, this was the order of the events: they first heard the apostolic teaching about Christ; then, through further instruction about the deeper roots of Christianity, they came into contact with the prophets. They received the "prophets" through the service of "the apostles."

This new type of Gentile Christianity which starts growing rapidly about the middle of the second century cannot take for granted the acceptance of the prophets as part of some common religious/ethnic heritage but rather must consider it as a second step following a first step of believing in Christ. Thus Justin considers "the prophets" as a "second-hand possession" received through the mediation of the apostles. But he adds in the same breath that the apostles transmitted the prophecies together with their authentic meaning—a meaning not available without faith in Christ. His thought is best summarized in this phrase:

> We believe in the voice of God uttered through the apostles
> of Christ and announced to us through the prophets.[108]

(b) Another important novelty in Justin's thought is the increased emphasis on "the apostles" as mediators of revelation whose teaching *remains accessible in written form.* His well-known passage about the Sunday liturgy juxtaposes "the memoirs of the apostles" with the "writings of the prophets" and unmistakably both expressions refer to literary works.[109] They constitute the material of readings during the celebration. The expression is quite significant: it not only restates Justin's customary order (apostles first, then prophets) but links closely the written Gospels (probably Matthew and Luke are meant)[110] with "the apostles," in fact more closely than we would have expected any ancient writer to link them together. He attributes the Synoptic Gospels to "the apostles" in general probably for the first time, but Irenaeus and later Tertullian follow suit eagerly. It is very unlikely that Justin would mean that these "memoirs" were in fact written by "apostles" as literary authors, i.e., that they were compositions of people belonging to the group of the Twelve. His expression seems to affirm two things. On the one hand, he indicates that the content of the Gospel narratives reached us through the mediating role of "the apostles," the first preachers of Christianity. On the other hand, he obviously associates these writings with the literary expression *apomnēmoneumata,* the genre of historical recollections known to antiquity. It is questionable whether the specific meaning of the literary genre should be pressed for obtaining the correct meaning of Justin's words.[111] Sources of the early second century are inclined to put the "apostolic teaching" in the context of recall, remembering, reminding, keeping in memory, etc.[112] It seems that Justin's choice of word (*apomnēmoneumata*) expresses the awareness that, in these writings, material first entrusted to memory has found fixed form of expression in writing. This interpretation corresponds well with the fact that it is in the middle of the second century that the importance of written records grows far beyond the traditional role of oral tradition. A few decades later, Irenaeus testifies that the written records play the leading role in any theological reflection or debate and thus the final shaping of the New Testament canon becomes imperative.

F. *The Synthesis of St. Irenaeus*

When taking a stand against the mushrooming Gnostic movements of the second century, the bishop of Lyons did not create a purely defensive position on behalf of traditional doctrine. His *Adversus haereses* is a major attempt to formulate a theological synthesis which answers the Gnostics in a comprehensive way by satisfying the needs and solving the problems that caused the Gnostic movement. It is not our purpose here to point out the place of Scripture in the Irenaean synthesis. Elsewhere I have attempted to show that Irenaeus has formulated a "theology of Scripture" which is an integral part of his synthesis.[113] Yet before we ask Irenaeus about his thought concerning the canon, we must emphasize that the backbone of his synthesis is the thesis of a unique and unified salvation history which comprehends all mankind by leading it to one and the same God the Father through one and the same Logos by imparting the one and same Spirit.

Irenaeus sees the Scriptures as the products of this salvation history, issued from it in its different phases. He routinely refers to "the prophets and the apostles," not only as mediators of revelation in Old and New Testament but as two collections of writings.[114] Occasionally, he uses a bipartite formula for the New Testament, speaking about "the Gospel and the apostolic doctrine" or the "teaching of Christ and the apostles."[115] These together with "the prophets" form the "triptych" we have spoken about in connection with Ignatius and Polycarp.[116]

There is little doubt that apostolicity is the main criterion for Irenaeus for holding any Christian doctrine as binding. Similarly, he considers normative "the apostolic writings" and treats them as divine word, equal in dignity with the Old Testament.[117] Although he would refer to the Gospels he accepts (the "tetramorphous Gospel" of Matthew, Mark, Luke and John) as "Gospels written by the apostles,"[118] he knows well that two of the four were not written by apostles but by "apostolic men," disciples of the apostles.[119] He carefully points out the Petrine "apostolicity" of Mark's Gospel and the close ties between Paul and Luke.[120] Most probably "these close ties" are partly (mostly?) reconstructed from Acts and the Pauline letters[121] but possibly also from traditional statements coming to him from Papias and Justin.

He takes issue with the Gnostics on behalf of the fourfold Gospel claimed by the Church. It is in this connection that his position of a closed canon appears: all the four are apostolic and hence normative and no other Gospel qualifies as such. One must be careful in evaluating the aprioristic argument that Irenaeus brings up to demonstrate that there must be no more or less than four Gospels. His argument should not be taken in isolation from what he holds about apostolicity. Since he knows of no more or fewer apostolic Gospels[122] than the four he lists, he presents the allegorical interpretation of Ezekiel's vision of the four cherubs (Ezek 1:4–21) standing for the fourfold Gospel.[123] Such "arguments" are in full harmony with the theory of allegorical interpretation. They are "aprioristic," that is, deductive, only in the sense that they want to demonstrate the existence of a divine intention "from of old" and its fulfillment as the realization of a divine and everlasting plan. In some sense, Irenaeus gives here the "ultimate reason" to the question: Why four Gospels? But we should not think that his closure of the Gospel canon rests entirely or even principally on this allegory. It is an allegorical approach to demonstrate that the factual arrangement of salvation history *as known from other sources* had been well established in God's intentions long ago. But knowledge about it is obtained differently: it is through the application of the principle of apostolicity that he (and with him the Church) is able to see that there are four valid and normative Gospel accounts.

The principle of apostolicity makes Irenaeus see the canon as *de facto* closed even if he does not attempt to give an exclusive list of all the apostolic writings. For him, the apostolicity of the books is a *quaestio facti* for which the Church is able to give reliable information. But the question is of course necessarily directed to the past. Newly composed books have no chance of being considered for the canon.

Nowhere does Irenaeus state that the prophetic and apostolic writings contain all of God's revelation or that they would constitute the exclusive channel through which God's word could be learned. Occasionally, he even states the contrary by showing that the eventual lack of availability of such books is no necessary hindrance for the word of God to spread, since the authentic proclamation of the Church can supply the link between the apostles and the post-apostolic times. In other words, at least in principle, Irenaeus' concept of apostolic tradition is wider than his concept of apostolic Scriptures. However, for all practical purposes, when he wants to ascertain the apostolic teaching about any particular question, he turns to Scriptures by using practically those same books that figure in the canon of the Church in later centuries.[124] Thus, while he considers the *paradosis* of the apostles as a living process of oral transmission which does not necessarily result in an adequate written expression, he turns for arguments of undisputed apostolic authority to the books that he accepts as apostolic. So, his practice of theological reasoning shows his awareness of a canon *de facto* possessed by the Church, a canon of books with a special (near to exclusive) role of transmitting the apostolic tradition. He comes to this position mostly because of Gnostic pressures. The Gnostic claim of "secret apostolic tradition," a different use of the same apostolic principle that Irenaeus believes in, can be successfully rebuked only if he is relying on apostolic tradition well published in the past.[125] His clinging to the New Testament books is the safest measure of excluding any apostolic tradition that had not been demonstrably handed over to the Church in earlier times.

Irenaeus carefully coordinates his position about the *apostolic writings* with his doctrine of apostolic succession and his teaching on inspiration. Without taking these into account, we cannot understand the coherence and validity of his thought.

For him, the visible and tangible structures of the Church are co-extensive with the realm of the Spirit's active presence in the world. Consequently, he postulates the influence of the Holy Spirit active within the historical framework of "the prophets and the apostles" (Old and New Testament) extended through the chain of legitimate apostolic succession into the life of the Church. For the Church to be an authentic extension of the original community started by the risen Christ, he demands that it be ostensibly in historical continuity with the organization started by the apostles. In this understanding of the Church, crucial importance is attributed to the so-called "apostolic Churches" founded by the apostles like those of Asia Minor, Greece and, most importantly, Rome, the place where Peter and Paul were active.[126] These churches witnessed in their institutional structure the transition from the first beginnings of Christianity to later generations. Irenaeus sees in them the social structures within which continuity of tradition is assured. The passages of the *Adversus haereses* about "elders" who saw some of the apostles are important for Irenaeus, for he can point to them as the concrete persons through whom the link of apostolic tradition reaches back to the threshold of the apostolic age itself.[127] For the "apostolic Churches," not only an uninterrupted chain of doctrine and office is guaranteed but "the safeguarding of the Scriptures without tampering, their full retention without addition and subtraction, their uninterpolated text as well as their legitimate and careful interpretation avoiding both

danger and blasphemy."[128] Irenaeus definitely means historical continuity which at such Churches would guarantee the extant memory
of the apostolic teaching and thus safeguard continuation and consistency against any possible deviation caused by malice or human frail-
ty. As the text quoted above shows, this safeguard of continuity
works for him as an historically demonstrable factor assuring not
only the authenticity of the canonical books but their uninterpolated
texts as well. Irenaeus' famous allegorical explanation of the "fourfold Gospel"—the establishment of the necessity of four Gospels, no
more and no less, based on the text of Ezekiel—has been quoted often as a proof of his basically non-historical mentality in such matters.[129] But the use (or better: abuse) of that passage is largely unfair.
Irenaeus makes it abundantly clear that for him the chief criterion of
normativity is apostolicity. Only after having settled the issue of the
apostolicity of the four Gospels does he indulge in allegory to ex-
plore, by scrutinizing God's eternal plan and sovereign will, possible
reasons of symbolic order for such a status of facts. But—and on this
we must insist—in his anti-Gnostic position, he settles the issue of
apostolic claims (those of the Gnostics vs. those of the anti-Gnostic
churchmen) with an historically conceived argument which explains
the authenticity of the Church traditions held as apostolic on the basis of Church structures reaching back to apostolic times. The authenticity of the apostolic writings as possessed by the apostolic
Churches fits into this argument.

It is true, however, that Irenaeus' last word does not consist of
claims of historical continuity. It is the permanent presence of the
Spirit in the Churches—those Churches linked with the apostolic origins through succession of doctrine, of sacramental life and of episcopal office—that guarantees the permanence of truth for doctrine,
the canon of Scriptures and the method of exegesis.[130] Irenaeus' reasoning leads ultimately to an ecclesiological view: true teaching is the
gift of the Holy Spirit and it can remain intact only as a consequence
of the Spirit's influence filling the Church. Since Church structures
are always animated by the Spirit—i.e., the inspiration originally giv-
en to the apostolic Churches remains alive for all successive generations—the permanence of truth (truth also concerning the
Scriptures) is guaranteed.

Thus we might summarize by saying that, for Irenaeus, the criterion of canonicity is the apostolic character of the writings. For this he does not require actual apostolic authorship. Certainly, he tries to bind the Gospels of Mark and Luke (and Acts) as closely to Peter and Paul as possible. In doing so, he uses traditional material. Yet, especially in the case of Luke, he pushes the argument for apostolic (Pauline) authenticity as far as possible—many would say, way beyond what is plausible. However, in principle, he requires "apostolicity" only for what content these books offer and consciously admits books written by non-apostles into the canon. The apostolicity of the major Churches is for him an argument to refer the question of the apostolic origin of these books to the Churches that continually existed since their apostolic foundations. While the argument has a sound historical plausibility—at least in principle—which is increased by the factual harmony of the major apostolic Churches in such matters of tradition, Irenaeus does not base the ultimate credibility of Church teaching on historical proofs alone. His demand of faith for what the apostolic Churches teach is not based only and ultimately on the claim that the apostolic Churches factually preserved unchanged traditions and texts but on the claim that the Holy Spirit given by Christ originally to the apostolic Churches has been preserved according to God's purpose and with his assistance. The permanence of the Spirit causes the permanence of true doctrine, authentic Scriptures and valid interpretations as long as the Churches stand in demonstrable continuation of succession with their apostolic beginnings.

G. *Conclusion*

1. SUMMARY

Let us retrace the path we have followed from the earliest layers of the New Testament tradition to the works of Irenaeus in reconstructing the beginnings of the canon of the New Testament. No matter how fragmentary our information is, no matter how partial and incomplete our investigation, it seems that we succeeded obtaining the pattern of a continuous development. It starts with the earliest Christian community holding only the writings of the Old Testament as Sacred Scripture and leads to the firm grasp of a new set of apostolic writings by the Church, a set of writings set beside (and theologically on top of) the old Scriptures. This development happened in four consecutive phases.[131]

(a) *The apostolic phase,* from Jesus to the destruction of the temple in 70 A.D. In this phase, the Church possesses only the "law and the prophets" as Scriptures. But it interprets them in the light of the teaching, delivered by qualified and authorized messengers, about Jesus, the risen and glorified Christ.

(b) *The subapostolic phase,* from the destruction of the temple to the Bar-Kochba revolt in 135 A.D. In this period the Church collects written expressions of the apostolic teaching of the past and sees a multiplicity of efforts to create a written record for the apostolic teaching orally transmitted during the previous phase. The Pauline epistles get collected; the Synoptic traditions become enshrined in coherent and full narratives; Pauline traditions get included into deutero-Pauline epistles with various adjustments and extrapolations according to the changing needs of a growing Church. The Johannine writings receive their final shape and form. The Church consciously adheres to the norm of "the prophets and the apostles," the first meaning the Scriptures of the Old Testament, the second meaning the apostolic tradition available in both oral and written form.

(c) *The phase of rising Gnosticism* between the Bar-Kochba revolt and the death of Justin Martyr in 165 A.D. The Church is culturally cut loose from its Jewish origins. Gentile Christianity emerges; for it the Old Testament writings appear as a "mixed blessing." The Gnostic movement seeks to meet the spiritual needs of the age and uses the Christian sources of teaching for constructing a system of "gnosis," i.e., a system of self-understanding built into a universalistic religion focusing on the understanding of the inner man and the spiritual cosmos to which he belongs. For obtaining such a deepening of Christian beliefs, some try to exploit the Old Testament by bold and radical attempts of allegorism; others use it eclectically and mix its data with cosmological speculations, while others, like Marcion, try to eliminate the Jewish records by identifying them with the "evil principle" of a dualistic system.

In this context, the Church needs to assert its recognition of a Christian gnosis as a legitimate aim, retain the Old Testament as an integral element of revelation and the historical background of

Christian salvation history, and further develop the christological exegesis of the Old Testament texts according to the principles and
practices of the apostolic traditions.

In this period of transition, the principle of apostolicity emerges
as the key issue. Basically all parties concerned recognize this principle. Gnostic groups claim that their esoteric systems are based on secret traditions originally entrusted to one or several apostles. (One
must observe that the idea of secret tradition, entrusted to some—
not all—of the apostles, already foreshadows the Marcionite option:
siding with one apostle against the others.) At this time, various attempts are made to blend the Gospel narratives into one coherent
and consistent presentation. This in itself does not appear objection-
able. Marcion builds his system in this historical context by choosing
Paul and rejecting all other apostolic sources. When doing this, he
distorts Christian data for the sake of his dualistic views and resolves
the contradictions found between the various traditions. Perhaps
most importantly, he gets rid of the Jewish ballast.

In this epoch, Justin stands out as the man best equipped to see
and remedy the crisis of the Church. He is a philosopher capable of
incorporating Hellenistic views and concerns into a comprehensive
salvation history by appealing to the omnipresent Logos always affecting human history. He applies allegory but seriously values the
foundations of history so that he can both confront the claims of
Jewish exegesis and hold to the Jewish roots of the Old Testament.
He shows the central role of the apostolic tradition; he is aware of
the fact that the Synoptic material read at the liturgical functions
perpetuates the data entrusted to the memories of the first preachers.
He is the first to combine the principle of apostolicity with reliance
on written records. Although his statements envisage only Gospels
(almost certainly Matthew and Luke, probably also Mark, with some
probability John), his assessment of the role of the written records of
the apostolic traditions becomes the most important guideline for the
anti-Gnostic synthesis formulated in the last decades of the century.

(d) *The anti-Gnostic phase,* from Justin to Irenaeus (and to his
later contemporaries, Tertullian, Clement of Alexandria and Hippolytus of Rome). It is characterized by the clarification of what is or is
not acceptable for the bishops of the major centers of Christianity,
or, we might say, by the polarization of the Church into Gnostic and

anti-Gnostic fronts. Step by step the anti-Gnostic theologians assure their foothold in older tradition and spread out their combat in unified terms over the whole empire. We have reviewed above only Irenaeus' synthesis. The bishop of Lyon marks a major milestone in the development of the canon. The later anti-Gnostic authors contribute further details of some importance but in the basic issues they agree with Irenaeus.

Irenaeus takes over and deepens the doctrine about the Old Testament as Christian possession. He sees that the principle of apostolic tradition must practically mean adherence to apostolic writings possessed and interpreted in the context of an apostolic Church. His stand against secret apostolic traditions logically leads him to shift all questions and arguments to scriptural debate. He cannot clarify the witness of the apostolic sources without quoting the apostolic writings. Thus for him the authenticity of the apostolic writings possessed by the Church and the falsehood of the Gnostic documents becomes a crucial question. He finds his answer with the help of historical considerations, turning to the apostolic Churches, witnesses of the change from oral to written tradition. But his argument receives ecclesiological depth as he asserts that the Holy Spirit permanently present in the Church's divinely willed and apostolically established social structures is the ultimate guarantee of truth, a guarantee commensurate to the act of faith expected of Christians.

Irenaeus' concept of canonicity, based on apostolicity, is historically imperfect and inaccurate but is far from being naive. At least in the case of Mark and Luke, he clearly shows his awareness of the role that others than apostles have played in writing the apostolic Scriptures. He is aware, in particular, of the importance of the "disciples" of the apostles in the transition period from apostolic to post-apostolic times. He asserts the providential role of the Holy Spirit guiding the process of the recording, at times even with regard to the verbal formulations found in the documents. While he knows (or suspects) fewer subtleties and complications along the process producing the allegedly apostolic writings than modern historians would, he clearly relegates the question of apostolic authenticity to the judgment of the Churches of apostolic origin. In general, he equally attributes ultimate authority to "the Scriptures of the apostles," "the churches of apostolic origin" and the Holy Spirit. But when the question of judging the authenticity of the scriptural texts directly surfaces he simply relies on what the apostolic Churches hold as norm, and he attributes their concordant judgment to the one same Spirit equally present in all such Churches.

2. REMARKS AND QUESTIONS

For the development of the New Testament canon, each of the four phases played a definite role, and each presents a number of unresolved questions.

(a) The apostolic phase formulated for the first time a message that gave radically new meaning to the Jewish Scriptures. Thus, the roots of a New Testament lie here. The possibility and need of new Scriptures, which, however, do not cancel the validity and importance of the Old Testament, grew out of the first proclamation about Christ, presented as the Messiah "according to the Scriptures." That this message was, already at the beginning, a matter of authorized proclamation appears clearly from both the evidence of Paul's self-understanding as an apostle and the semitic roots of the concept of apostleship in the Synoptic tradition. However, there is a great deal of obscurity about the precise meaning of the term "apostle" and the exact distribution of leadership roles. The list of the Twelve so faithfully reproduced in Matthew, Mark, Luke and Acts stands in contrast with the small amount of information we know about the individuals named. Furthermore, it must be remarked that the Johannine Gospel and the three Epistles of John avoid the use of the term *apostolos,* although the Fourth Gospel mentions the Twelve and their election by Jesus as a matter of presupposed knowledge on the part of the reader. If the word *apostolos* is a household word in Christian communities at the turn of the first century, why is it never mentioned in the Fourth Gospel?[132] The passage about the twelve apostles of the Lamb as the twelve portals of the heavenly Jerusalem shows the fundamental importance of the concept of apostleship at about that same time. Similar conclusions can be drawn from the use of the term in Luke, Acts, Ignatius and 2 Peter; the first decades of the second century are certainly permeated by awareness among Christians about the founding role of the "apostles" even if the term is used with fading historical features and growing theological schematization. Thus we can hardly find an answer with precision to the question: To what extent did the first Christian generation perceive the Christian message as "the preaching of the apostles"? How did the blending of historical information with theological schematization take place as the time span and geographical distance rapidly grew between the "first believers" and the changing Church?

We might also state with definite clarity that the change from oral message to written documents has occurred as a process whose roots reach back to the apostolic age. But the time and way of solidifying the oral tradition into permanent formulas, narratives, blocks of unchanging material, entrusted to memorization, and then to written documents, are only a matter of conjecture. We may assume the importance of the Pauline letters in this process as models for depositing apostolic teaching in a permanent form. We might see in the Synoptic passion narratives the first block of solidified apostolic tradition destined to unchanging preservation. In any case, there is enough evidence to take seriously the connection between the apostolic leadership of the first Christian community and the written heritage surfacing in the last decades of the first century. We cannot easily dismiss the second century's claim of continuity with the apostolic past as fictitious. Although the details are often beyond historical reconstruction, from an overall vantage point we must be impressed seeing that Paul's statement about the "pillars of the Church" in Galatians (Gal 2:9) almost literally corresponds to what the canon-makers of the second century saw when they assembled, besides the collection of Pauline letters and a Gospel narrative "somehow" connected with Paul (Luke, with Acts as a second volume), Petrine material (Mark, 1 and 2 Peter), Johannine writings (John, Revelation, 1, 2 and 3 John) and books connected with Jewish Christianity associated with James (Matthew, James and Jude). It is hardly imaginable that this one verse of Galatians led all such efforts or that the resulting canon coincides only by chance with what Paul reports about the leadership of the early Church. It is much more reasonable to conclude that the leaders of Paul's time had, indeed, a long-lasting impact on the Church which, in due process, gave birth to writings still connected with their names. One is inclined to agree with Irenaeus that if there were "apostolic Churches," that is, Church communities with uninterrupted ecclesial life between the apostolic and the anti-Gnostic phase, then it appears to be plausible that the permanence of the Church structures gave historical basis to the permanence of apostolic doctrine expressed at due time in written documents.

(b) The second, or subapostolic, phase sees the process of "Scripture making" increase and produce the last portion of the New Testament writings. We know very little about the process resulting in the deutero-Pauline letters.[133] Our knowledge of the *Redaktionsgeschichte* of Luke and John is much too tentative for giving answers about the respective roles of authentic traditions, the new needs of the Church and the more or less pious attempts of extrapolation and/or falsification along the process. One might ask if 2 Peter would not be a most candid case of pseudepigraph allowing us to obtain the best insights into the social and psychological background producing posthumous apostolic literature. The authors, redactors and collectors of the sacred books are the ones most active in solidifying the model of "apostolic origins" into a "theologoumenon" which certainly has historical basis, although, concerning the details, this basis remains somewhat vague. When they edit and finalize their understanding of the apostolic past they already anticipate in their activities a closed canon. The closure of the canon is a later development only in the sense that it makes explicit what is already implied in the activities of the "Scripture makers." We may wonder about the actual contacts Irenaeus had with the presbyters of Asia and the influence he received from the Church of Rome through visits and correspondence.[134] But, doubtlessly, he represents well the implied logic of the activities that took place by his elders (in both senses of the word, "presbyters" belonging to the previous Christian generation) as he decided to set apostolicity as the criterion of a closed canon.

We must mention here the meaning of the enigmatic figure of Papias who stands at the borderline between a devotion to the "living voice" or oral tradition and his interest in the apostolic credentials of the written documents. The fragments preserved from him certainly testify to the force with which oral tradition still asserts its role at his time and how much the Church needed guidelines to make final judgment about the apostolic authenticity of various documents already in circulation. He represents well the subapostolic age as a period engaged in coordinating the attempts of "remembering" with efforts of "listening to the Spirit." That he does not see yet the solution in possessing a comprehensive set of inspired Scriptures, held and interpreted by an inspired Church (a Church filled with the Holy Spirit), is not surprising. From his perspective a synthesis is not yet visible because written tradition has not come to occupy a sufficiently pervasive role.

(c) The Gnostic phase reveals the weakness of the subapostolic Church oscillating between oral and written norms while temporal distance from apostolic origins is growing further. The openness of the Valentinians to draw from all traditions is just as dangerous as the single-minded Paulinism of Marcion. While all parties concerned pay lip service to the principle of apostolicity, these dangers become visible. The idea of "secret apostolic traditions" grants free entrance to any teaching. In this situation we discover weakness in the ambiguity of the Church's position adhering to "apostolic traditions" without, however, determining them precisely. The casual mixing of different Gospel traditions can produce as much uncertainty as the position of Marcion which disqualifies the Twelve for their alleged falsification of the genuine teaching of Jesus. But most disturbingly, the quest of the Gentile Christians for gnosis—a deeper understanding of the self and of the cosmos—clashes with the limited ethnic perspectives of the Jewish Scriptures and the sober (mostly moralizing) ancient Christian exegesis.

The Gnostic phase makes the old clinging to oral tradition untenable and urges the Church to find a new approach to the interpretation of the Old Testament. Justin's teaching is, to a great extent, a fitting remedy. But he has a very partial collection of apostolic writings. The lack of the Pauline corpus in his repertoire is his greatest handicap. We might forever wonder what Justin thought of the Pauline writings. But without them, he was unable to establish claims to full possession of the apostolic heritage and all its written expressions, and, consequently, was unable to give full answer to the problems raised.

We do not know at what time and in what fashion the co-existence of the various Gospels took its beginning in the various Churches. We also lack sufficient evidence for the needs and claims that made Tatian and possibly others (Basilides?) produce a unified

Gospel narrative. It appears probable that Marcion's first success in the Church of Rome is connected with the fact that adherence to only one Gospel narrative was in itself not regarded as heretical. However, the exclusiveness of Marcion underlying the Marcionite canon revealed itself as disruptive because it created a growing number of conflicts with the Church and stimulated it to assert the validity of the different sources carrying authentic apostolic traditions in the Church. While the sub-apostolic Church made the implicit decision of a closed canon, it was in the Gnostic phase that the Church reached out for the possession of a full canon, the complete possession of all apostolic teaching and thus of all apostolic writings. While in this phase Marcion dramatizes the problem, Valentinus, combining the different traditions, anticipates the direction to which the anti-Gnostic Fathers were about to move.

One may wonder if it was the Gnostic movement that motivated the Church to set certain models of what an acceptable "apostolic writing" was supposed to be. In retrospect, it is obvious that the New Testament basically consists of Gospel narratives and apostolic letters. Exceptions are few and do not deviate too much from these standards. Acts is, after all, the continuation of Luke, and the other exception, Revelation, itself contains seven letters. Documents like the *Didache* never make it to the canon. No prophetic book other than Revelation is accepted as canonical. (Of course it is also of epistolary form!) The Muratorian canon rejects Hermas' prophetic book because "the prophets" (the Old Testament) constitute a closed collection (*completo numero*), while the book cannot be put among the apostolic books either since it is obviously too recent. Would the Book of Revelation have ever become canonical without its alleged Johannine origin? The question is hard to answer. It seems that the Church knew how to identify as "apostolic books" those it needed. And, of course, it did all this on the basis of its convictions that it possessed in its apostolic foundations all that was needed to build upon. We do not know when and how the apostolicity of the writings became associated with the expectation of certain literary genres. One might, however, rightfully suppose that the historical tradition, associated with the Synoptics in the way we find it in Papias, and the widely spread and reliable tradition about Paul as a letter writer, known to Clement of Rome, the author of 2 Peter and Ignatius, had a decisive role in creating the assumption that authentic apostolic writings must be Gospel narratives or epistles. Nevertheless, this criterion of the literary genre never appears in the early Church as decisive, or seldom is it ever consciously applied. But from the final outcome of the development of the canon we might reasonably assume that as a first "screening" device, it was employed to *disqualify* quickly other forms of literature since there was no reliable tradition that the apostolic Church had produced any other kind of literature than these two types. The Epistle to the Hebrews is the most impressive argument for this assumption: according to all probability it was given an ending making it resemble a Pauline epistle and so a possible candidate for apostolic origin. The fact that both Revelation and Hebrews nevertheless remained for some time "of doubtful canonicity" fortifies the argument.

(d) The anti-Gnostic phase is best known from its end result. Less known is the way in which Irenaeus' answer to the major problems raised by the Gnostic crises found a resounding echo within a few decades all over the major Churches of the empire. We can suppose the existence of multiple contacts among the Churches. The central position of the Roman Church is conjectured from the trips made to Rome by Polycarp, Marcion, Valentinus and later Irenaeus. But already in the previous phases Ignatius and Paul traveled to Rome and documented their concern for obtaining favorable reception by writing letters preparing their arrival. As a Church taught by both Peter and Paul, the Roman community stands out as an apostolic Church of special distinction. Its role is of crucial importance for Irenaeus who is the first to assign consciously a pivotal role to the apostolic Churches. Searching for an explanation of the success that Irenaeus' synthesis met in the Church throughout the empire, one of the reasonable assumptions would be that through the Roman Church both the major Gnostic movements and their anti-Gnostic counterparts found an easy road into the other urban centers of the empire. There is no way of overrating the cultural importance of Rome as capital in the first two centuries of our era. The influence was due to constant communication between the imperial capital and the provinces. Through the Church of Rome, there has been, therefore, constant communication connecting also the Churches of the provincial capitals. Yet the synthesis of Irenaeus would not have become common possession within such a short period of time, had he not presented a doctrinal synthesis richly drawing from traditions already present in all major Church centers. Irenaeus' manifold ties with Asia Minor also well explain his closeness to the cities containing the largest number of Christians in the second century. His dependence on Justin and Papias shows that he has consciously worked for a synthesis that unites the various traditions of the major Christian centers. But we must also remember that Asia Minor and Rome had their doctrinal exchanges before the time of Irenaeus. Polycarp's visit to Rome during the reign of Anicetus is one of the memorable events of this sort. It is most probably one of numerous similar contacts. Also between the Churches of Rome and Alexandria many contacts must have taken place, even if only a few are recorded. But the speed with which Valentinianism found its way from Alexandria to Rome should give us an idea about the facility with which the teachings of Justin and Irenaeus could have found their way to Alexandria. It appears to be ironic that Catholic/Protestant debates about Roman primacy usually concentrated in the past on different alleged or supposed functions of the bishop of Rome with respect to other Christian Churches and easily ran into pure speculation because of lack of documentation, while here we see an area of definite Roman influence spreading the tradition of the apostolic Church of "Peter and Paul" without evidence of explicit Roman claims to establish the canon of sacred books for other Churches. The function of Rome appears in the context of our topic mostly as a factual unifying influence transmitting in an "ecumenical fashion" the respective traditions of the apostolic Churches, combining and connecting them by aiming toward fullness and completeness and thus counteracting the Gnostic alternatives that either introduced foreign elements with a syncretistic eagerness or adopted one tradition to the exclusion of others.

3. Epilogue

In the synthesis of Irenaeus I see a position that is both theologically valid and ecumenically exemplary. It was the leading light for the Church's understanding of the Scriptures for at least one thousand years. Even beyond the Middle Ages, it has continued to exercise its influence until the present day. In Catholic theology following the Second World War, it has again obtained extraordinary influence through the patristic renewal usually associated with names like Yves Congar, Jean Daniélou, Henri de Lubac and Hans Urs von Balthasar. I am convinced that Irenaeus was one of the patristic figures most vigorously present at the Second Vatican Council inspiring a theological vision centered on salvation history and focusing on universality, pastoral concerns and ecumenical sensitivity.

It seems, however, that the theological validity of Irenaeus' thoughts about canon and apostolicity are not sufficiently recognized. First of all, we must see that his principle of apostolicity as applied to the canon is basically a statement about *the original authenticity* of the writings of the New Testament. As it does not state actual apostolic authorship, it affirms nevertheless that the writings of the New Testament contain in written form the first message delivered by the first messengers of Christianity and they have therefore inherited the same normativity that must be ascribed to the first witnesses empowered by the risen Christ for their ministry of teaching. This theological idea cannot be abandoned without abandoning canonicity itself, without relinquishing Scripture as Scripture. Furthermore, Irenaeus sees clearly that the *quaestio facti* (the judgment about the apostolicity of particular books) is an issue partly historical but ultimately transhistorical and therefore it should be responded on two levels. His argument about the living tradition of the apostolic Churches, as a credible witness of reliable information about the apostolic origins of the particular books, makes good sense in such general terms. And Irenaeus in fact does a good job reporting traditional views that connect the various crucial parts of his canon with the leading personalities of the apostolic Church. There is no logical fault with his reasoning: the Church precedes the New Testament Scriptures both logically and historically. The apostolic Churches— local Churches with institutional permanence reaching back to the first Christian generation—are reasonably conceived as sensors capable of comparing their present-day holdings with the original teaching they had received. Yet the role of the Church transcends the task of historical preservation or the task of certifying historically the identity of what is taught now and what the original teaching was. Were its task only historical (evaluation of identity of doctrine according to set philosophical or cultural patterns), we could re-examine it at any time in the light of later but better equipped research and, in view of philological and historical discoveries, rewrite the canon. In this case, the judgment of Irenaeus' Church could be invoked as deserving some historical credibility but it could by no means demand the commitment of faith. However, Irenaeus knows better, also. The judgment of the Church is not simply based on its ability to "remember" its origins through a chain of interconnected officials. It is the possession of the Holy Spirit that guides the Church to pass correct judgment about the documents of faith, a judgment that can be defended or made plausible by historical arguments but cannot be proven beyond doubt by invoking the reliability of human memory. And, in fact, Irenaeus sees that the judgment of the apostolic Churches about both doctrinal issues and the composition of the canon states *conformity,* and not verbal or logically deducible identity. He knows that only in possession of the Spirit can the Church propose its Scriptures and demand faith in them, demand the response man owes to God and God alone.

Irenaeus' theology of the canon leads us, therefore, as any theological investigation of canon and canonicity should, to questions concerning our basic beliefs and concepts about the Church, the heart of ecclesiology.

NOTES

1. The oldest extant list of the sacred books of the New Testament is found in the *Muratorian Fragment,* usually dated at the end of the second century. The basis for this dating is the statement it contains about *The Shepherd* of Hermas: "The Shepherd was written most recently in our times (*nuperrime temporibus nostris*) in Rome by Hermas, while Pius, his brother sat on the episcopal seat of the Church in the city of Rome": edition by M. Meinertz, *Einleitung in das Neue Testament,* (Paderborn, 1950) 323. This dating has been challenged by A. C. Sundberg, "Canon Muratori: A Fourth-Century List," *HTR* 66 (1973) 1–41. He assigns to the word "nuperrime" the meaning of "lastly" and explains "temporibus nostris" as referring to our times in a theological sense: the last phase of the history of salvation. Thus, in his interpretation "nuperrime temporibus nostris" can refer to an event that occurred one hundred and fifty years earlier. The weakness of Sundberg's hypothesis is twofold: (a) it is clearly motivated by a theological pre-conception, for a closed canon does not fit into his scheme of evolutionary development before the fourth century; (b) he does not provide us with any example according to which "nostra tempora" can mean in early Christian Latin a theological epoch without chronological implications. There is, therefore, no reason for us to understand the text in any way other than its obvious meaning, viz., the fragment cannot be dated later than a generation after the episcopate of Pius (142–155), i.e., the end of the second century.

2. A brief survey of Irenaeus' views about Scripture is presented in Denis Farkasfalvy, "Theology of Scripture in St. Irenaeus," *Revue bénédictine* 78 (1968) 319–333.

3. Origen strongly depends on Justin, Irenaeus and Clement of Alexandria. His differences from Irenaeus and Clement with regard to canon and interpretation must not be overemphasized at the expense of his close ties with them, based, as it seems, on their common anti-Gnostic cause. Henri de Lubac points out a special anti-Marcionite thrust: "c'est surtout aux positions de Marcion et de son disciple Apelles que parait s'en prendre la prédiction d'Origène." Cf. *Histoire et esprit. L'intelligence de l'Écriture d'après Origène* (Paris: Aubier, 1950) 53.

4. Most insightful are the quotations assembled by Y. Congar in his

Tradition and Traditions (New York: Macmillan, 1967) 30–42. Pierre Grelot also, when reviewing the problem of the canon during the anti-Gnostic period, concludes: "Variations of detail do not lessen the importance of this substantial agreement between Asia Minor (represented by Irenaeus who originated there), Rome (Clement and Hippolytus), Africa (Tertullian to be followed by Cyprian) and Alexandria (Clement and Origen)." *The Bible, the Word of God* (New York: Desclée, 1968) 153.

5. See for example R.M. Grant, "The New Testament Canon," *The Cambridge History of the Bible*, ed. by P.R. Ackroyd and C.F. Evans (Cambridge: Cambridge University Press, 1970) Vol. I, 284–307.

6. "In spite of the nebulous character of the evidence relating to the synod of Jamnia, it is difficult to doubt that . . . (the canon's) precise contents had been settled soon after A.D. 100, if not earlier": G.W. Anderson, "The Old Testament. Canonical and Non-Canonical," *The Cambridge History of the Bible* I, 135. Both the comparison of the variety of literature represented by the Qumran discoveries with this final canon settled around 100 A.D. and the evidence of a larger selection of Old Testament books transmitted through early Christianity show that at the turn of the second century rabbinical Judaism was in no mood to widen the collection of sacred books. At the same time, Christians were engaged in a process of expansion leading to a canon containing, in addition to the entire collection of Jewish books, later fixed as "the Jewish canon," the deuterocanonical books of the Old Testament and, of course, the whole New Testament.

7. *Marcion and the New Testament. An Essay in the Early History of the Canon* (Chicago: University of Chicago Press, 1942).

8. *Die Entstehung der christlichen Bibel* (Tübingen: Mohr, 1968). English translation: *The Formation of the Christian Bible* (Philadelphia: Fortress, 1972).

9. Marcion's method of finding "antitheses" (contradictions) is apparently not restricted to the Old Testament. Finding the record of opposition between Peter and Paul in Galatians 2:11, he invented his theory of irreconcilable division among Paul and the Twelve. The unwarranted extrapolations based on this one verse are rightly pointed out by Tertullian, *Adv. Marc.* 1.20.2–3 (CCL I, 461). Tertullian is also quite aware of Marcion's ultimate concern and motivation which are not his Paulinism or interest in historic authenticity but rather of a philosophical nature: "an unhealthy interest in the question of evil" (*ibid.,* 1.2.2; CCL I, 443).

10. I use the term "euaggelion" in its Pauline sense. Paul's conviction both that there is only one "euaggelion" and that it becomes multiple only by distortion is expressed in the first chapter of Galatians: "I am amazed that . . . you are going over to *another Gospel. But there is no other.* Some

who wish *to alter the Gospel* of Christ must have confused you" (Gal 1:6–7). This agrees with Tertullian's position as he speaks "de unitate praedicationis." Cf. *Adv. Marc.* 1.20.4 (CCL I, 461). The original oneness of the kerygma appears to be challenged by the hypothesis of H. Koester, "One Jesus and Four Primitive Gospels," *Trajectories through Early Christianity* (Philadelphia: Fortress, 1971) 158–204. He does not attribute enough weight to Galatians 1:6–7. A pluralistic "Gospel" at Paul's time would have undermined his position which should have appeared, in that case, as contrary to the nature of the Christian movement. But there is no evidence that either Paul or his opponents were aware of a pluralistic concept of Christian origins in which the multiplicity of the Gospel would have been considered as legitimate.

11. "Delivered" and "received" in v. 3 describe the process of tradition in the early Church. Cf. C.H. Dodd, *The Apostolic Preaching and Its Development* (New York: Harper, 1944). More specifically about this verse see H. Conzelmann, *I Corinthians* (Philadelphia: Fortress, 1975) 250. Conzelmann thinks that the Scriptures referred to in the passage "can only be Hos 6:2" (*ibid.* 256). For divergent opinions see note 12.

12. Our contemporary tendency to water down the Old Testament ties with Christian data by denying the role of specific passages is well expressed in a recent commentary: "Probably *according* to the Scriptures must finally be taken as having a general reference; and specific passages supply not precise exegetical support but phraseology adaptable to the Christ data believed by the early Christian Church": W.F. Orr and J.A. Walther, *I Corinthians* (The Anchor Bible 32; Garden City: Doubleday, 1976) 321. The threefold repetition of "according to the Scriptures" is not explained if Paul is dealing only with "phraseology."

13. It can be questioned whether the image presented of Paul in Acts, approaching in each city first the synagogue and only afterward preaching to the pagans, corresponds to historical events or is only a schematization ill-fitting for "the apostle of the Gentiles" (Rom 11:13). Cf. E.P. Sanders, "Paul's Attitude Toward the Jewish People," *USQR* 33 (1978) 175–187. See "A Response" by K. Stendhal, *ibid.* 33 (1978) 189–191. Certainly, in his argumentation in Romans 10:14–21, Paul supposes that the preaching of the Gospel was to be addressed first to Israel and only after being rejected by the Jews was it offered to the Gentiles. Cf. also Rom 1:16 and 2:10.

14. For the early Church's view on the Old Testament as prophecy cf. R.E. Brown, "Hermeneutics," *The Jerome Biblical Commentary* (Englewood Cliffs: Prentice Hall, 1969) 610–612.

15. Cf. also 1 Cor 10:11. It expresses the same theological position.

16. Recently, Bo Reicke, in *The Epistles of James, Peter and Jude* (The

Anchor Bible 37; Garden City: Doubleday, 1964) 71, presented arguments in favor of an early date, preceding the death of Peter about 65 A.D. This position is by no means universal. Cf. G. Kümmel, *Introduction to the New Testament* (Nashville: Abingdon, 1966) 292–299. For an early date, see also Joseph A. Fitzmyer, "The First Epistle of Peter," *The Jerome Biblical Commentary* 362–363; also John A.T. Robinson, *Redating the New Testament* (Philadelphia: Westminster, 1976) 140–169.

17. Hebrews 1:1–4 summarizes and generalizes this position.

18. I do not necessarily imply that "the Book" opened by the Lamb is indeed the collection of writings that constitute the Old Testament. However, it is quite likely that the symbolism of "the Book" includes the prophetic meaning of the old covenant with its people, history and holy Scriptures as a whole. Thus the opening of the Book by Christ implies that he makes the ultimate meaning of the Old Testament appear. Cf. J.M. Ford, *Revelation* (The Anchor Bible 38; Garden City: Doubleday, 1975) 94.

19. Cf. T.W. Manson, *Mission and Message of Jesus* (New York: Dutton, 1938) 633–634, and *Studies in the Gospels and the Epistles,* ed. M. Black (Philadelphia: Westminster, 1962) 22.

20. R. Laurentin, *Structure et théologie de Luc I–II* (Paris: Gabalda, 1957) 64–92. Cf. R.E. Brown, *The Birth of the Messiah* (Garden City: Doubleday, 1976) 241–245.

21. Luke 11:49. On the origin and interpretation of this verse, see Denis Farkasfalvy, " 'Prophets and Apostles': The Conjunction of the Two Terms before Irenaeus," *Texts and Testaments* (San Antonio: Trinity University Press, 1980) 111–112.

22. Cf. V. Taylor, *The Gospel According to Saint Mark* (New York: Macmillan, 1966) 472. More recent research on this parable is assessed by C.E. Carlston, "Parable and Allegory Revisited: An Interpretive Review," *CBQ* 43 (1981) 228–242.

23. I refer here to the Jesus tradition of the Gospels and presuppose a dating of all canonical Gospels not significantly earlier than 70 A.D. Of course, St. Paul's letters and, possibly, 1 Peter are of earlier origin.

24. Neither the question of the so-called "testimonia" (proof texts from the Old Testament collected for the purpose of Christian missionary activities) nor the problem of the earliest logion collections has been resolved with sufficient certainty. However, the frequency of the same Old Testament passages appearing in early Christian texts dated to the last decades of the first century gives us enough basis to suppose the existence of quotation lists. As far as the logion collections are concerned, besides the finding of the *Gospel of Thomas* among the Nag Hammadi writings, the terms in which the Synoptic problem appears justify the supposition that such collections actu-

ally existed. At this point we need no other fact to work with than the simple existence of this kind of literature. About the "testimonia" cf. B. Lindars, *New Testament Apologetic* (Philadelphia: Westminster, 1961).

25. Even by restricting ourselves to the letters whose Pauline authenticity is accepted virtually by all scholars (Rom, Gal, 1 Thess, Phil, 1 Cor, 2 Cor and Phlm) it is clear that Paul's letter writing was occasioned by a multiplicity of circumstances and motives. However, Romans stands out as a literary work quite different from the rest. Its purpose is not that of following up on the results of previous missionary activities. It appears to be the earliest example of a Christian literary work that attempts to present the Christian message in a comprehensive manner and in confrontation with both paganism and Judaism. Joseph A. Fitzmyer calls Romans "a letter of introduction" fashioned as "an extended exposé of (Paul's) understanding of the Gospel": "The Letter to the Romans," *The Jerome Biblical Commentary,* 291. By the fact that Paul did not know personally the community addressed and also because he addresses them with full awareness of his apostolic authority, we can say that in this work he comes closest to the consciousness of "writing Holy Scripture," i.e. of presenting a message received from God with an authority conferred by God to a community of believers beyond his actual reach.

26. With due openness to attempts at an early dating and to the idea of Matthean priority, I work with the supposition that the composition of Matthew and Luke (with Acts) is posterior to 70 A.D. and that Mark is probably the earliest Gospel extant. I see no evidence for the existence of any similar literary work prior to 60 A.D., although the existence of earlier logion collections or isolated narratives is probable.

27. The theme of the suffering prophets of the Old Testament is relatively frequent in early Christian documents. Jas 6:10 and Heb 11:32 are good examples. The *Ascension of Isaiah* testifies to a strong need and interest among Christians at the turn of the first century to re-create the historical model of the Old Testament prophets more in line with the suffering of Jesus and the martyrdom of the apostles. Cf. especially chapter 4 (vv. 2–3) in which Isaiah predicts the martyrdom of "the twelve apostles": E. Hennecke and W. Schneemelcher, *New Testament Apocrypha* (London: Lutterworth, 1963) 303.

28. Cf. Denis Farkasfalvy, " 'Prophets and Apostles': The Conjunction of the Two Terms Before Irenaeus," *Texts and Testaments* (San Antonio: Trinity University Press, 1980) 109–134.

29. What is only implicit in Matthew's ending is here a consciously made statement: the book as a written document is destined to perform the task usually assigned to oral preaching and teaching—building up faith in

Jesus as the Christ and the Son of God and thus providing divine life for the believer.

30. I consider definitely pseudepigraphic 2 Peter, Jude and the Pastorals. Such designation is doubtful for Ephesians and Colossians. 2 and 3 John constitute a special case. Not the production but the reception of these documents appears to be based on something similar to pseudepigraphy. The confusions developing about the identity of "the presbyter" writing these letters as well as the identification of John son of Zebedee with the author of Revelation and with the presbyter promoted the inclusion of these books into the canon although there appears no conscious effort on the part of the writers to produce "apostolic letters" written in the name of John the apostle. The relationships between the apostle, the "beloved disciple," "the presbyter" of 2 and 3 John and the seer of the Apocalypse remain veiled in mystery. Cf. R.E. Brown, *The Community of the Beloved Disciple* (New York: Paulist Press, 1979) 31–34, 93–97.

31. For a dating about 150, the arguments are well collected by W. Marxsen, *Introduction to the New Testament* (Philadelphia: Fortress, 1968) 245. Reasons for an early dating are presented by Bo Reicke, *op. cit.,* 144. My dating follows Isidor Frank, *Der Sinn der Kanonbildung* (Freiburg: Herder, 1971) 177: with extensive German literature.

32. "Clinging" to the apostles is an affectionate term used by Ignatius in reference to Christian origins. But he does not cling to them as an historian of our times would. The complete phrase reads: "Being inseparable from God, from Jesus Christ, from the bishop and the precepts of the apostles" (Trall 7:1). There can be no doubt that, for Ignatius, God, Jesus Christ, bishop and apostles are themselves inseparable terms.

33. Cf. W.F. Arndt and F.W. Gingrich, *A Greek-English Lexicon of the New Testament and Other Early Christian Literature,* 2nd ed. (Chicago: University of Chicago Press, 1975) 356. Efforts of earlier generations to interpret our text with an active meaning of inspiration find little echo in present-day scholarship. For this antiquated position see H. Cremer's article in *Realenzyklopädie für protestantische Theologie und Kirche,* ed. A. Hauck (Leipzig: Hinrichs) 9, 184.

34. Some authors assessing the doctrine of inspiration in the Old Testament find this state of affairs disturbing: practically all the statements of the Old Testament about inspiration refer to divine action upon the *oral* proclamation of a message. "Seemingly, then, the doctrine of the inspiration of the Scripture, as it is understood in the Church today, is not mirrored in the writings of the Old Testament": R.F. Smith, "Inspiration and Inerrancy," *The Jerome Biblical Commentary,* 500.

35. Almost twelve centuries later, St. Thomas Aquinas still deals with scriptural inspiration within the context of prophecy. His later disciples usually deplore the lack of distinct concept of biblical inspiration in his thought without realizing that he presents a point of view tied with age-old teaching about the history of revelation. For a recent treatment of scriptural inspiration from an historical perspective cf. Bruce Vawter, *Biblical Inspiration* (Philadelphia: Westminster, 1972).

36. The terminology of biblical inspiration becomes differentiated only at the end of the Middle Ages. In fact, the term "inspiration" is not used in any technical sense to designate the inspiration of the Bible before the seventeenth century. Cf. Denis Farkasfalvy, *L'inspiration de l'Ecriture sainte dans la théologie de saint Bernard* (Rome: Herder, 1964) 42–58.

37. The concept of "theologoumenon" appears frequently in German literature. Typical is its use by Isidor Frank: "Es kann dabei kein Zweifel sein, dass es sich beim Begriff des Apostolischen, insbesondere des Zwölfapostolates, um ein kirchliches Theologoumenon handelt": *Der Sinn der Kanonbildung* (Freiburg: Herder, 1971) 204. I use this concept, however, without supposing that a theologoumenon is necessarily ahistorical. I treat "apostolicity" as a concept well rooted in historical facts but theologically simplified and reinterpreted in post-apostolic times.

38. 1 Clem 42:1–4. Interesting is Clement's insistence that the succession of apostles by bishops and deacons is no innovation but carries out provisions foretold by Is 60:17. This reflects a theological mentality in search of scriptural proofs for any controversy, Scripture meaning, of course, the Old Testament.

39. "The apostles received *the Gospel* for us from Jesus Christ" (*ibid.*). "What did he (Paul) write to you in the beginning of the gospel?" (1 Clem 47:2). This usage is strictly Pauline: "apostle" means "being set apart for the Gospel" (Rom 1:1).

40. Peter and Paul are mentioned in 1 Clement 5, Paul alone in 47:1.

41. That the apostolic preaching was delivered "with the conviction of the Holy Spirit" is stated in 1 Clem 42:3. More significant is the statement of 1 Clem 47:2 about Paul writing "truly in an inspired way" (*pneumatikōs*) because it designates the Pauline letters as inspired writings. For Clement "Sacred Scriptures are true and given by the Holy Spirit" and therefore must be studied (45:2). This last statement closely repeats what we found in 2 Tim 3:16.

42. The testimony of Peter and Paul described in 1 Clem 5:45 stands in the context of a list of Old Testament examples among whom Moses and David are also mentioned. The specific point of comparison is persecution

motivated by jealousy. Peter and Paul stand out in martyrdom as leaders since "to these men who lived holy lives there was joined a great multitude of elect"; allusions to the persecution of Nero follow.

43. Clement quotes the writing of Paul to document the previous record of dissent among the Corinthians. While doing so, however, it becomes clear that Paul's admonition given once in the past possesses lasting value since it was given by an apostle under inspiration. It is a quotable instance amid a large number of Old Testament passages which are, in fact, quoted before and after as prophetic and inspired texts. We see that his theology of apostleship enables Clement to use a Pauline text analogously to the way in which he uses the Old Testament.

44. Examples: "For the Holy Spirit says," followed by Jer 9:23–4, then: "Above all, remember the words of the Lord Jesus which he uttered while teaching forbearance and patience," followed by a free rendering of Matt 5:7; 6:14–5 and 7:12. This is continued by the words "the Holy Logos says" at an introduction to Is 66:2 (1 Clem 13). A similar sequence is found in 1 Clem 46:1–8.

45. The explicit quotation of 1 Cor 1:10 in 1 Clem 47:3 takes place after a string of Old Testament passages introduced by "it is written," and the phrase "Remember the words of the Lord Jesus, for he said" introduces a conflated version of Matthew 26:24 and Luke 17:1. Finally we read: "Take up the letter of the blessed Paul, the apostle." This structure becomes in the patristic age the classic format of theological argumentation: Old Testament Scripture followed by the words of the Lord and confirmed or expounded by an apostolic witness. When studying its use in St. Bernard of Clairvaux, I called attention to the traditional character of this "triptych" of revelation: prophets–Jesus–apostles. Cf. Denis Farkasfalvy, *L'inspiration de l'Ecriture sainte dans la théologie de saint Bernard* (Rome: Herder, 1964) 107.

46. Time and again Old Testament texts are attributed to Christ as the speaker: Ps 21:7–9 (1 Clem 16:15), Ps 33:12–18 (1 Clem 22:1–7), Ps 140:5 and Job 5:17–26 ("the holy Logos says": 1 Clem 56:5–15). Elsewhere the Spirit is said to be speaking of Christ in the biblical texts as, for example, in Is 53:1–12 (1 Clem 16:3–14).

47. Clement's "moralism" is an obvious result of such an exegetical approach.

48. Cf. R.M. Grant and H.H. Garden, *First and Second Clement* (The Apostolic Fathers 2; New York: Nelson, 1965) 10–11.

49. Eph 11:12.

50. Philad 5:1; Trall 2:3; Magn 6; Smyrn 8.

51. *syndesmos apostolon,* Trall 3.

52. Smyrn 3.

53. Magn 13.

54. About the "Gospel" meaning Jesus Christ in a personal yet comprehensive sense, see Philad 9:1–2.

55. This claim of the Old Testament's validity appears with emphasis in Magn 8:2 and 9:3. He also says that "the prophets anticipated the Gospel in their preaching" (Philad 5:2).

56. "The decrees of the Lord and of the apostles" (Magn 13:1); "cling inseparably to God Jesus Christ, to the bishop and to the precepts of the apostles" (Trall 7:1).

57. The most explicit passage is found in the letter to the Philadelphians: "Your prayers to God will make me perfect so that I may gain that fate which I have mercifully been allotted, by taking refuge in *the Gospel* as in Jesus' flesh and in the apostles as in the presbytery of the Church. And the prophets, let us love them, too, because they anticipated the Gospel in their preaching" (5:1–2). This text contains the "triptych" mentioned above (note 45) in reference to Clement of Rome.

58. Phil 9:2.

59. Phil 5:1.

60. Did 1:3b–4a. This section, called often an "interpolation," is a clearly defined block of Synoptic material that has possibly entered the *Didache* at a later stage of its redaction. Cf. R.A. Kraft, *The Didache and Barnabas* (The Apostolic Fathers VIII; New York: Nelson, 1964) 60–61. This possibility does not lessen the validity of our conclusion that in the *Didache* Christian morality is presented in two isolated sets of precepts, the first taken from the apostolic tradition, the second from the Old Testament.

61. Behind this conjecture there lies a number of unsolved problems. Up to and including Justin Martyr the Synoptic material appears with openness to conflations and variations. Cf. A.J. Bellinzoni, *The Sayings of Jesus in the Writings of Justin Martyr* (Leiden: Brill, 1967) 139–142. I think that, besides the customary references to a free flow of oral tradition, we must realize that before the canonical status of the New Testament books became established it is anachronistic to expect that they be quoted *verbatim*.

62. *Op. cit.*, 67.

63. Eph 2:20 and 3:5.

64. 1 Cor 12:28–29.

65. This evaluation supports a "later" dating of the *Didache* (first half of the second century) but does not exclude that it might contain earlier material.

66. Bar 16:35 shows that the temple site is in ruins. Consequently, the

work in its present form must have been written after the destruction of 70 A.D. but before the erection of Hadrian's pagan temple in 135 A.D. Cf. R.A. Kraft, *op. cit.,* 42.

67. Bar 5:8–9.

68. Bar 8:3–4. This passage contains an important phrase: "he (Christ) gave them (the apostles) *the authority of the Gospel.*" Kraft's translation seems to be correct as he renders the text: "he entrusted them the authority to proclaim the Gospel" (*op. cit.,* 105). The phrase implies the principle of apostolicity by attributing to the apostles a special gift for presenting the Gospel with (divine) authority.

69. See our remarks about the anonymity of the apostles earlier in this section.

70. It seems that Paul's program to appropriate the Old Testament as Christian Scriptures, as mentioned earlier, remained only a program with no satisfactory execution until, to say the least, the time of Origen. Many theologians might be inclined to agree that this program never found satisfactory implementation.

71. Kraft made up an impressive list of Barnabas' "Gnostic-parenetic" terminology. (*op. cit.,* 24–25) The word *gnosis* itself occurs eleven times in the document and is treated as the result in the believer of the exegetical process.

72. As in many other Christian texts, *pneuma* is not only the Spirit of God but also that of man, his "gnosis receiving faculty" (cf. R.A. Kraft, *op. cit.,* 26).

73. Bar 1:7; 5:6; 5:8–9; 6:10. It is in such a context that we find the "triptych" of the history of revelation: prophets–Jesus–apostles (Bar 5:6–12).

74. Bar 9:7; 6:14; 12:2; 14:9.

75. The words *allegoria* or *symbolon* are absent from Barnabas. But he uses *typos* ten times and *parabola* twice (Kraft, *op. cit.,* 25–26).

76. The Gnostic concepts of apostleship need further investigation. Similarly, there are many open questions concerning the literary genre of a "Gospel" as conceived in the first two Christian centuries. It may not be as univocal as the canonical Gospels indicate. However, it remains a fact that the Gnostics often attributed their documents about deeds and/or teaching of Jesus to apostles (Peter, Paul, John, James, Thomas and Philip appear in the Nag Hammadi manuscripts). But, of course, the specifically Gnostic claim of "secret traditions" often led the Gnostic authors to choose one of the women belonging to Jesus' inner circle as the alleged transmitter of the revealed material in question. Thus we have *The Gospel of Mary: The Nag*

Hammadi Library, ed. by James M. Robinson (New York: Harper and Row, 1977) 471–474. Such Gospels are unacceptable to the anti-Gnostic Fathers who, like Irenaeus, insist that all of Jesus' revelation was made public by the apostles.

77. "Letter of Ptolemaeus to Flora": W. Foerster, *Gnosis. A Selection of Gnostic Texts* (Oxford: Clarendon Press, 1972) 154–161. The document is from about 160. It quotes also Paul twice with a similar formula.

78. J.M. Robinson, *The Nag Hammadi Library,* 51. According to the editor of this document, Malcolm L. Peel, "the author seems to be a late second-century Christian Gnostic who is certainly influenced by Valentinianism" (p. 50).

79. *Extraits de Théodote* (SC 23) 14:1 (p. 87), 35 (p. 136), 49 (p. 163), 67 (p. 191), 85 (p. 209). It is not clear if Eph 4:10 or Jn 3:13 is referred to by "the apostle says, indeed," *ibid.* 7:4 (p. 71).

80. The expression *monogenēs* is attributed to "the apostle" in 7:3 (p. 68). John 1:9 is quoted with the formula "the apostle says" in 41 (p. 149).

81. In 13:3, Theodotos quotes 1 Pet 1:12 as "Peter said" and then continues quoting verse 18 with the formula "according to the apostle" (p. 82).

82. Cf. 74 (p. 197).

83. The formula occurs also in *The Treatise on Resurrection* I, 4: "indeed, as the apostle said," continued by quotation of Rom 8:17 and Eph 2:5–6 (*The Nag Hammadi Library,* 51). The Valentinian ties of this writing are not quite sure. It might be, however, from the later decades of the second century.

84. These data contradict H. von Campenhausen's claim that Paul is the apostle *par excellence* throughout the second century "among Catholics as well as among Marcionites and Valentinians," in *The Formation of the Christian Bible* (Philadelphia: Fortress, 1972) 143. M.C. Boer in his "Images of Paul in the Post-Apostolic Period," *CBQ* 42 (1980) 359–380 tries to show that such a view of Paul is already present in Colossians and the pastorals. However, there is little evidence that Paul was considered *the only apostle* by anyone before Marcion. From our examples, it is also obvious that quoting Paul as *ho apostolos* does not necessarily imply such a designation; *per se* it only means that the quoted text is backed by apostolic authority.

85. Cf. above. Characteristically, the apostles are treated by the *Muratorian Canon* and by the *Epistula Apostolorum* as a group acting in unison. The latter states, "John and Thomas and Peter and Andrew and James and Philip and Bartholomew and Matthew and Nathanael and Judas Zelotes and Cephas (!), we have written to the churches": E. Hennecke and W. Schneemelcher, *New Testament Apocrypha,* 193.

86. Epiphanius reports a Jesus-logion not included in any known Gospel: "He who spoke in the prophets is I, I who now stand before you": A. Resch, *Agrapha* (TU 30; Leipzig: Hinrichs, 1906) 207. It seems to be based on Is 52:6.

87. *The Gospel of Thomas* 52, trans. by T.O. Lambdin (*The Nag Hammadi Library*, 124).

88. While the Valentinian connections of Ptolemy (n. 77) and of Theodotos (n. 79) are certain, they are not as sure for the *Treatise on Resurrection.* Cf. Bentley Layton, *The Gnostic Treatise on Resurrection from Nag Hammadi* (Chico, Cal.: Scholars Press, 1979) 4–5.

89. "There are contacts with all four Gospels. . . . The fact that the Johannine material is shot through with Synoptic phrases, and the Synoptic with Johannine usage, permits the conjecture that the author knew all and every one of the canonical Gospels": J. Jeremias, "Papyrus Egerton 2": E. Hennecke and W. Schneemelcher, *New Testament Apocrypha*, 95. Cf. also F.-M. Braun, *Jean le théologien dans l'église ancienne* (Paris: Gabalda, 1959) 89–94. H. Koester has recently challenged this position by defending an earlier date (about 120) for the document and denying its dependence on John: "Apocryphal and Canonical Gospels," *HTR* 73 (1980) 105–130.

91. Cf. F.-M. Braun, *op. cit.*, 112–113. He dates it between 140 and 150. George MacRae prefers to speak about the second half (or the middle) of the second century (*The Nag Hammadi Library*, 37). Kendrick Grobel dates it between 140 and 170: *The Gospel of Truth* (Nashville: Abingdon 1969) 27. W.C. van Unnik's thesis about Valentinus' authorship, " 'The Gospel of Truth' and the New Testament," in F.L. Cross, ed. *The Jung Codex* (London: Mowbray, 1955), is generally not accepted, although see the recent treatment by Benoit Standaert, "L'Evangile de Verité: critique et lecture," *NTS* 22 (1975/76) 243–75.

92. I find the remarks of H.E.W. Turner quite helpful in assessing the role of Marcion in the development of the canon: "It seems altogether most probable that Marcion offered a premature though clear-cut solution to a problem of which the Church was already cognizant and to which it was already beginning to frame an answer. It might even be maintained, without transgressing the element of half-truth involved in paradox, that Marcion was not so much a reagent as the precipitate of the quest for canonicity within the Great Church." And further: "The selection of Marcion as a decisive factor in the development of the Christian canon of Scripture does less than justice to the complexity of motives, part domestic and part external, which contributed to the result": *The Pattern of Christian Truth. A Study in the Relations Between Orthodoxy and Heresy in the Early Church* (London: Mowbray, 1954) 243–244.

93. R.M. Grant, *Gnosticism and Early Christianity* (New York: Harper, 1966) 121–128.

94. "Languens enim—quod et nunc multi, et maxime haeretici—circa mali quaestionem, unde malum, obtusis sensibus ipsa enormitate curiositatis inveniens creatorem pronuntiantem: 'ego sum qui condo mala' ": *Adv. Marc.* 1.2 (CCL I, 443).

95. We must remark here that the figure of Paul quickly forgotten and then in need of rediscovery is part of the hypothetical panorama depicted for the second century by Walter Bauer in his *Rechtgläubigkeit und Ketzerei im ältesten Christentum* (1st ed. in 1934) whose English translation, *Orthodoxy and Heresy in Earliest Christianity* (Philadelphia: Fortress, 1971), still exercises considerable influence. Cf. D.J. Harrington, "The Reception of Walter Bauer's *Orthodoxy and Heresy in Earliest Christianity* During the Last Decade," *Harvard Theological Review* 73 (1980) 289–298. For further correctives see also H.E.W. Turner, *op. cit.*, 169–172.

96. See below and note 101.

97. The formula in 2 Clement is somewhat different: *kai ta biblia kai hoi apostoloi* (2 Clem 14:2). It can be translated as "both the Bible and the apostles" (say). *Ta biblia*, of course, refers to the Old Testament, while *hoi apostoloi* means the revelation of the New Testament in both oral and written transmission.

98. H. von Campenhausen, *The Formation of the Christian Bible* (Philadelphia: Fortress, 1972).

99. J. Knox, *Marcion and the New Testament* (New York: Abingdon, 1946).

100. The question can be formulated in this way: Why and when did Luke's two volumes (Gospel and Acts) become separated by the insertion of the Fourth Gospel into the canon? However, one might see, as I am more and more inclined to do, in Luke's two volumes the germ of the canon of the New Testament. They comprise, on the one hand, a Gospel that intends to congregate in an orderly and comprehensive fashion all available material about Jesus and include also, on the other hand, the apostolic teaching by presenting their deeds and speeches. Approaching Luke's work in this way, we would see that the canon makers of the second century proceeded along the same line: for the sake of a full presentation of the Jesus-tradition, they embedded Luke's Gospel into a collection with three other works and then continued his presentation of the apostolic tradition by a collection of apostolic letters. If the canon of the New Testament needs a single person as its initiator, then this distinction should go to Luke rather than to Marcion.

101. Philad 6:3.

102. It is our single source from which we might conclude that Marcion

called his Scripture *euaggelion kai apostolikon*. It is, however, possible that Epiphanius reflects here a Marcionite terminology which does not go back to Marcion himself.

103. Cf. *Adv. Marc.* 4.2.1 (CCL I, 547).

104. Tertullian refutes Marcion from Marcion's own Scripture. Thus in his *Adversus Marcionem* the Pauline epistles appear in the same order as in Marcion's canon. In Book V he reviews Galatians as the first piece of Marcion's apostolikon: *Adv. Marc.* 5.2.1 (CCL I, 655).

105. *Adv. Marc.* 4.39.6 (CCL I, 651–2); 5.17.6 (716). Cf. also Irenaeus, *Adv. haer.* 3.5.3 (CCL 211, 360).

106. *Stromata* 1.13.5 (GCS 52, 10); 4.132.1 (306–7).

107. *Marcion and the New Testament,* 29.

108. *Dialogue with Trypho* 119, 6.

109. *First Apology* 67, 3.

110. Justin's use of Mark is debated but seems to be probable. There are more doubts about his possible use of John. The possibility that all he used was a Gospel harmony is less vindicated.

111. Cf. R. Heard, "The *apomnemoneumata* in Papias, Justin and Irenaeus," *NTS* (1954/55) 122–129.

112. The theme of remembering is frequent in early Christian literature dealing with the apostles: 2 Pet 1:13–15; 3:2; Jude 5 and 17; 1 Clem 46:8 and 47:2. R. Heard, in his article quoted above, shows that both Justin and Irenaeus depend on Papias in whose fragments (Eusebius H.E. 3.39) the word "remember" occurs four times.

113. Denis Farkasfalvy, "Theology of Scripture in St. Irenaeus," *Revue bénédictine* 78 (1968) 319–333.

114. The texts are frequent: "He who called us through the apostles from every place, called those of old through the prophets": *Adv. haer.* 4.36.5 (SC 100, 901). Cf. also 3.19.2 (SC 211, 367); 3.24.1 (SC 211, 470); 4.32.5 (SC 100, 865).

115. "From the rest of the Lord's doctrine and the apostolic letters": *Adv. haer.* 5, Preface (SC 153, 12); "from the apostles and the sermons of the Lord," *ibid.* 2.2.5 (Harvey I, 257). In *Adv. haer.* "Dominus et Apostol*us*" is a reference to Marcion's Scriptures: 1.25.2 (Harvey I, 219).

116. Frequently the "triptych" of salvation history occurs in the writings of Irenaeus: "as the Lord gives witness, the apostles proclaim it and the prophets preach it": *Adv. haer.* 3.26 (SC 211, 338). Cf. also 3.6 (SC 211, 64); 3.9.1 (SC 211, 98); 5 Preface (SC 153, 10); 5.26.2 (SC 153, 334). Slight variations appear in 2.40.2 (Harvey I, 348) and 2.58.2 (Harvey I, 387).

117. Best indications are the passages referring to the same Spirit speak-

ing through the prophets and the apostles. Cf. *Adv. haer.* 3.21.4 (SC 211, 408).

118. "Revertamur ad eam quae est ex scripturis ostensionem eorum qui et evangelium conscripserunt Apostolorum": *Adv. haer.* 3.5.1 (SC 211, 52). The Gospel was "handed over to us by the apostles": 3.11.9 (SC 211, 174). In this last text, remarkable is the mixture of the "Gospel" with "Gospels" as Irenaeus insists on the unity of the message and the plurality of its form but excludes the validity of any more than four Gospels.

119. *Adv. haer.* 3.1.1 (SC 211, 224).

120. Luke was "inseparable from Paul": *Adv. haer.* 3.14.1 (SC 211, 258). "At all these events Luke was present and described them carefully": *ibid.* (SC 211, 261). "He was a companion and a co-worker of the apostles (plural!) without any jealousy transmitting to all people everything they have heard from the Lord. In the same way, he transmitted to us without jealousy all that he has learned from them:" *ibid.* 3.14.2 (SC 211, 266).

121. Cf. R. Heard, *art. cit.,* 128–129.

122. Irenaeus makes reference to the four Gospels as "apostolorum evangelia" or "illa (evangelia) quae ab apostolis tradita sunt"; "only these are true and well established" (*vera et firma*) *Adv. haer.* 3.11.2 (SC 211, 174). In Irenaeus, the anonymity of the apostles often disappears but only to give place to formulas like "Peter and John and Matthew and Paul," obviously the list of the "apostolic authorities" which stand behind the four canonical Gospels: *Adv. haer.* 3.21.3 (SC 211, 408). One might ask if the order of the canoncial Gospels is, in any way, fixed for Irenaeus. In the above quotation the order appears as "Mark, John, Matthew, Luke" but in *Adv. haer.* 3.11.8 the order is "John (lion), Luke (ox), Matthew (man) and Mark (eagle)," an order that was later changed—together with the symbolism of the creatures—by Church tradition. C.F. Grant thinks, however, that the order of this latter text, present already in Rev 4:7, represents the earliest tradition about the chronology of the four Gospels in reverse order: *The Gospels, Their Origin and Growth* (London: Faber, 1957) 65–67. We can add another—different—order of the four Gospels appearing in Irenaeus as he lists his scriptural arguments taken from the four Gospels: Matthew (III,9,1–3); Luke (III,10,1–5), Mark (III,10,6) and John (III,11,1–7). This is the order in which he examines each work for its origin and veracity.

123. *Adv. haer.* 3.11.8 (SC 211, 160–170).

124. Irenaeus' program in his *Adv. haer.* is clearly a scriptural one: to present proofs "ek tôn euaggeliôn kai apostolikôn" (the totality of the New Testament Scriptures). Cf. I.3.6 (Harvey I, 92). The plurals of both Greek nouns have an anti-Marcionite edge. Furthermore, Irenaeus wants to restore

the correct interpretation of the Old Testament by recognizing its prophetic character: 3.25.1 (SC 211, 408).

125. See the expression "without jealousy" in the passage quoted above (note 120). It means that neither the apostles nor Luke held back any part of the message revealed by Christ.

126. The most significant text is *Adv. haer.* 3.3.1–4 (SC 211, 30–44).

127. "Divinae inspirationis senior" (*ho theios presbyteros*) *Adv. haer.* 1.7.15 (Harvey II, 155); "senior apostolorum discipulus": 4.32.1 (SC 100, 796). He calls Polycarp "bishop constituted by the apostles": 3.3.4 (SC 211, 38).

128. This passage starts with the words "true gnosis." Irenaeus combines the "doctrine of the apostles" with the "ancient structure of the Church" (*antiquus Ecclesiae status*), the two being of equal status but of different nature as they function to assure "true gnosis" for the faithful; a third element is the succession of bishops: 4.33.8 (SC 100, 820).

129. "But Irenaeus' only concern is with the perfect symbolism. Four and no more, Plato's perfect number, is the number of cardinal directions, as we have noted": F.C. Grant, *The Gospels, Their Origin and Their Growth* (London: Faber, 1957) 66.

130. See the text quoted above (note 128). It combines the preservation of the authentic text with safeguard for correct interpretation.

131. Of course, the neat separation of these phases cannot be expected. Because of considerable geographic spread of the Church in an age of relatively slow communication, the successive phases sometimes overlap or follow each other in gradual transition.

132. This question is complicated by the fact that "the Twelve" are mentioned in John 6:67 and 70 with the clear supposition that the reader already knows that Jesus selected twelve disciples to form his "inner circle." Peter appears as their spokesman, and Judas, the betrayer, also belongs to the group. Although "the Twelve" are mentioned only once more in John (20:24), one naturally thinks of them as those who are with Jesus as his intimates in the second half of the Gospel, especially since both Peter and Judas are repeatedly named. In the discourses following the washing of the feet, Jesus speaks to them in terms of a special election which recalls John 6:70 (reference to *the election of the Twelve*) and with a terminology of mission, using the cognates of the noun *apostolos* (see esp. 15:16 and 17:18). However, it is the unnamed "beloved disciple" who is presented by this Gospel as the special witness guaranteeing the authenticity of its message. He is set in some kind of parallelism with clear elements of rivalry with Peter throughout the passion story. Their rivalry is resolved only in chapter 21, admittedly

a later addition to the Gospel. Cf. R.E. Brown, *The Community of the Beloved Disciple* (New York: Paulist Press 1979) 27–34.

It is hard to escape the impression that in the Fourth Gospel we find the traces of a development similar to what is found in Marcion. The Johannine Gospel singles out and emphasizes the role of the beloved disciple in opposition to Peter (and the Twelve in general) just as Marcion chose to set up Paul against Peter. The main difference is, of course, that in the Fourth Gospel the opposition between the beloved disciple and Peter remains tempered and is ultimately reconciled in an appended last chapter. Thus special importance is due to this appendix (chapter 21) in which, *under the theme of martyrdom,* Peter's superiority over the beloved disciple is proclaimed without, however, contradicting the claim of the previous chapters. Raymond Brown sees in the statements of chapter 21 the acceptance of the Petrine ecclesiology by the "Johannine community." (Cf. *op. cit.* 161–162.) For our specific topic, the importance of chapter 21, with its recognition of Peter (and the Twelve he represents), lies in the well-founded supposition that this appendix was needed for assuring the canonicity of the Fourth Gospel. Due to the appendix, John's ambiguity with regard to Peter and the Twelve is transcended: the "beloved disciple, as chief witness and the first believer" (cf. John 20:8) and possibly even the first disciple (see R.E. Brown's arguments about such an interpretation of John 1:35–40 in *op. cit.,* 32–34), cannot be regarded as the only reliable witness and faithful follower of Christ.

133. Most probably, this process is parallel to the formation of the *Pauline corpus* which, while being compiled, must have appeared to its collectors as lacking in many respects. Without indulging in speculations about the role of the pastorals for promoting certain hermeneutical trends, theological doctrines on Church order and apostolic traditions, we can still point out the importance of 2 Timothy, painting the image of Paul as the ideal martyr. This might have been needed for balancing the canonized tradition about Peter as a martyr. In fact, 2 Peter, written with the supposition that the apostle foresees his death (2 Pet 1:14–15), which, at the time of the letter's composition, is definitely known in the Church as the death of a martyr, indicates that there was a need of counterbalancing *this time* the image of Paul by that of Peter, equally blessed with ecstatic vision (1:17–18), predicting his martyrdom and thus matching Paul in wisdom (3:15–16).

For discovering the importance of martyrdom in the formation of the canon, I gladly recognize my indebtedness to Prof. William Farmer who stimulated my thinking in this direction.

134. W.H.C. Frend suggests that Irenaeus has visited Rome where he might have met Justin and Polycarp: *Martyrdom and Persecution in the Ear-*

ly Church (Oxford: Clarendon, 1965) 70–71. Of course, we have the record in Eusebius about his travel to Rome with the letter of recommendation by the surviving martyrs of Lyons (E.H. 5.4.1–2). His contact with Pope Victor in the quartodeciman dispute is also known.

INDEX OF TEXTS